Endorsements

Beverly Parrish is a veteran homeschool mom who has a breadth of experience that is hard to match. She has raised boys and a special needs daughter, and her children are already "rising up and calling her blessed!" She has been a mentor to many, many homeschool moms and has brought encouragement and wisdom to so many. She presents great information and insight in a compelling way. You will be inspired and blessed as you read her book ... and your children will thank you for it!

Tim Lambert, President
Texas Home School Coalition

Beverly Parrish adds incredible value to families in this book. Her vast experience navigating the pressures of homeschool life, the expectations of others, and the latest trends in homeschooling enable her to write with perspective. She brings counter-intuitive wisdom gleaned from the journey to adulthood with her children. These pages offer practical solutions for your current parenting challenges and an informed vision for the future.

Doug Bartsch, Pastor
HISplace Family Church

*In **Beyond the Diploma: Homeschooling with the End in Mind**, Beverly Parrish brings a no nonsense approach to all the complexities and considerations of homeschooling. Spoken with love and wisdom, she encourages those desiring to homeschool to reach for the stars while being planted firmly in reality. This is a must read if you want help to ensure that your child is purpose driven and emotionally and educationally intelligent in life.*

DENNIS MARK, EXECUTIVE DIRECTOR
REDEEMED MINISTRIES, HOUSTON, TX

A must-read primer for anyone considering or already engaged in homeschooling. A delightful and informative guide for those who not only want to educate, but enjoy the company of those closest to them: their children.

MARC SCHOOLEY,
CAROL AWARD WINNING AUTHOR OF *KÖNIG'S FIRE*

BEYOND THE DIPLOMA

Homeschooling with the End in Mind

By Beverly Parrish

Copyright © 2019
Beverly Parrish

Performance Publishing Group
McKinney, TX
All Worldwide Rights Reserved.

All rights reserved. No part of this publication may be reproduced, stored in a retrieval system or transmitted, in any form or by any means, electronic, mechanical, recorded, photocopied, or otherwise, without the prior written permission of the copyright owner, except by a reviewer who may quote brief passages in a review.

ISBN 13: 978-1-946629-45-6
ISBN 10: 1-946629-45-6

"Homeschooling wouldn't be so hard if you just didn't have to do it with your kids."

(Bev, October 30, 2010, 10:53 a.m.)

This book is dedicated to all the homeschool parents I've had the pleasure of meeting over these many years at conferences, book fairs, churches, libraries, and park benches. Sometimes, I was on the receiving end of your encouragement. Other times, you trusted me and shared your greatest fears and hopes. I am profoundly grateful that our paths crossed and that I count some of you as dear friends. You have enriched my life.

And to Chris, my maverick, who boldly leads our family with purpose, strength, and laughter. I am devoted to you always.

Contents

A Note from the Author 1

Chapter One: A Homeschool Fairy Tale 3

Chapter Two: Cast of Characters – The Story of Us 5

Chapter Three: A Fresh Wind Blows 11

Chapter Four: Take Inventory 15

Chapter Five: Get a Plan 19

Chapter Six: Adjust Your Expectations 29

Chapter Seven: Set Yourself up for Success 31

Chapter Eight: Taming Your Schedule 35

Chapter Nine: But What Do I Do Monday? 41

Chapter Ten: Survival Skills for the Real World – AKA Chores 45

Chapter Eleven: Choosing Curriculum that Fits 49

Chapter Twelve: How Much Does This Cost? 59

Chapter Thirteen: When Change Is Afoot 63

Chapter Fourteen: In Praise of the Ordinary 67

Chapter Fifteen: Survival of the Adaptable 73

Chapter Sixteen: Slow Down! Children at Play!..75

Chapter Seventeen: Homeschool Without Losing Your Family.........................81

Chapter Eighteen: To Train, or Not to Train, That Is the Question....................87

Chapter Nineteen: Moms and Boys, or Check Your Feminism at the Door......91

Chapter Twenty: Set Pinterest Aside..95

Chapter Twenty One: A Day in the Life 101

Chapter Twenty Two: Don't Give Up the Ship..105

Chapter Twenty Three: Abundant Life Homeschooling....................................111

Bibliography 121

A Note from the Author

I'm glad you've decided to join me. I consider it a privilege to be invited into your life to speak through these pages. It is my hope that you will leave here encouraged, inspired, and with a spring in your step. Are you tired of the frenzied pace you're keeping? If so, here are some questions for you:

Will all the things you've got going on right now get you what you expect at the end of this journey with your kids? Do you even know what you expect, or why you're doing this homeschool thing? I hope that I can help you clarify your answers to those questions. I have asked them myself, and I'd like to invite you to come along with me as we ponder them.

If we are unsure of our family's purpose in homeschooling our children, we have no clue as to how we should set our priorities. Our priorities determine how we spend our days. Those daily actions influence our family's path to the finish line. When we're not heading in a direction of our choosing, we're just blindly following culture. It takes intention and deliberate action to steer our families on a wise course, and I want to equip you to do just that. If I had to state our family's purpose in one sentence, it

A NOTE FROM THE AUTHOR

would be to raise great adults. Our personal definition of 'great' determined the focus of our homeschool efforts, and it has directed our decisions for almost 30 years now. My desire is to spur your thinking about all the possibilities for your family and the education of your children, and then equip you to define your family's purpose and act on it.

Let me state right up front that I'm a believer of Jesus Christ, and you will see that in these pages. However, the truths presented here are applicable to anyone. If you don't share my Christian viewpoint, I hope you'll still feel welcome to hang around. I believe you'll find something of value for your family as you take on this important task of educating your kids.

Chapter One

A Homeschool Fairy Tale

Once upon a time on a gentleman's small farm in Texas, there lived a mom and dad and two sons. This was a happy little family. Dad went off to work every day at his construction company. Mom stayed at home with the perfect boys and baked perfect cookies in her perfect apron and pearls. When the oldest boy was four years old, they dutifully enrolled him in a prestigious preschool program to assure that he would be properly socialized. Their son was, of course, brilliant. He stayed at that little private school through the end of kindergarten, when the school lost its lease and was no longer available. Mom and Dad quickly began searching for other options – other private schools, church schools, and the local public school. Panic had not yet set in, not until Mom mentioned the possibility of a fringe, commune, denim wearing, granola eating, hippie thing called *homeschooling* as a consideration.

Dad told Mom to just drop it, adding that it would take something like the audible voice of God before they ever homeschooled their son. But he did give the go-ahead to at least do some research about homeschooling, and after much reading on

Mom's part—giving Dad the Reader's Digest version of what she read, and a visit with the "voice of God" via Gregg Harris' Homeschooling Advanced Seminar—this little family decided that they would now homeschool their oldest son.

Neither set of grandparents was too pleased with the decision. Honestly, they didn't know anything about homeschooling, and in their defense, they just were concerned for the welfare of their grandchildren. But ignorance of the facts did nothing to quell their anxiety. The Mom came from a long line of public school teachers. There was even a school in a large Texas city named after her grandfather. Never fear, though, Dad stood firm in his conviction, and the decision remained. Because this happened in August, there wasn't much time to prepare before school started.

The Mom went to visit a friend who had great and vast experience in homeschooling. She had been at it for a year; she was an expert. She kindly offered to let Mom see the curriculum she used. Mom came, she saw, she ordered, and they began. After all, how hard could it be, right? That was almost 30 years ago. A few more kids were added to the mix, and they all lived happily ever after. Well, mostly.

Chapter Two

CAST OF CHARACTERS – THE STORY OF US

Just who are we? Chris and Bev Parrish are the mom and dad on that farm, married in 1982, seven great kids ages 34–17, living in a regular house in a regular subdivision in the Houston area. Just like you, we've had a motley assortment of pets as companions for our kids. Frank, Monty, and Hobbes were rather large snakes. There was Fuzzy the mouse that was supposed to be food for Hobbes but was nursed back to health and had a long mouse life. There were turtles, frogs, and a variety of rescued critters after hurricanes.

If you passed us on the street, you might not even notice that we're homeschoolers. We're ordinary. We've had no merit scholars, no star athletes, no music prodigies, no gifted linguists. Yep, just your average, everyday family. The one aspect that *might* make us extraordinary is that we're okay with being ordinary. That is not to say that we don't have high goals and ideals for our family, or strive for excellence in all that we do. It is to say that we've learned to relax and enjoy the process of life. Our

CAST OF CHARACTERS - THE STORY OF US

family has changed quite a bit since those days. Ben is married and has three children. Luke is also married. Andrew is married with three kids. Hannah, who has Down syndrome, is the princess of our story. Seth is out of the house and on his own. Gavin is serving in the Marine Corps, and Jack is finishing high school.

I write this book to communicate a passion of mine. Too often, I visit with homeschooling moms who are buried under fear, insecurity, dread, and anxiety over their job performance as homeschooling moms. To remedy this, they fill their lives with endless activity. I can only assume the purpose of such is to provide evidence of their good intentions should the homeschool police arrive at their door. Then it becomes a contest with friends over who has it the busiest.

It reminds me of the tales we gals tell one another of pregnancy and delivery. You know what I mean. When you're pregnant with your first baby, the other moms somehow feel obliged to tell you how they were in excruciating labor for twelve days before their fifteen pound baby was born two weeks late! Conversely, there will be plenty of moms to regale us with tales of their toddler reciting the multiplication tables and their 13-year-old who has just been accepted into medical school. We're glad for their remarkable kids, but wonder about the future of our own little ones who are mere mortals.

I have a passion to encourage us regular folks to relax and enjoy our ordinary lives. I have certainly not arrived. I'm not perfect and neither are my kids, but I do know one thing. It doesn't have to be as hard as we make it! When moms dissolve into tears as they tell me they are overwhelmed at the prospect of continuing to homeschool, my heart breaks. It ought not to be like that, and I want to encourage those moms to hang in there.

Parents, it's time to embrace God's call to each of us that directs us to a specific path, a path that's perfect for our individual, unique families. Bravely following our path and keeping our eyes on the Author and Perfecter of our Faith is our only hope for homeschooling with a peaceful heart and arriving at the right destination. I love this passage from *Let Go of Whatever Makes You Stop* by John Mason. "When you compare yourself with others, you will become bitter or vain for always there will be greater and lesser persons than yourselves."[1] We need to keep our eyes on *our* goal and run with endurance the race set before *us* – not someone else.

When we started homeschooling, there weren't many older women who had finished this race and could share their perspective from the other side of the finish line. Moms currently in the trenches readily shared their advice and counsel, which I deeply valued, but lots of them were actually my peers, rather than older women. I'll be bold and identify myself as an older woman. I don't have all the answers, but I've been around a while and I pay attention. I consider myself a student of life, specifically the life of a Christian family. In almost 30 years of homeschooling, I

---

[1] John Mason, *Let Go of Whatever Makes You Stop* (Tulsa, Oklahoma: Insight International, 1994), p. 57.

have listened to moms, and studied and watched the homeschool movement. I can offer some long-term perspectives.

Has our homeschooling experience been perfect and stress free? Oh my, no! I'm naturally wound up pretty tight as it is, and I like to do things the right way. When we began homeschooling, there were so few curriculum choices that practically everyone did the same thing. Extracurricular activities were limited. Co-ops and classes were virtually non-existent. As I said earlier, I made the well thought-out and agonized-over decision to use what my friend had used with her children.

Well, maybe I didn't think it over that well or spend much time in prayer. I mean, there was no time! For everything but math, we purchased a traditional, academically sound curriculum used in private Christian schools. The teacher's guides gave explicit instructions as to what to cover each day, even listing the specific flash cards we were to use with each lesson. Our math curriculum was scripted. Yes, that's right – scripted. It told me what I should say to my child, and what my child should do or say in response. We figured we'd struck gold! How hard can this be with these kinds of directions? It did hold my hand, which was essential. We were terrified that we'd mess up Ben. Consequently I followed the instructions to the letter. I mean exactly that. Okay, I did have the sense to realize that I couldn't organize a baseball game in my classroom to practice spelling words since it was only Ben and me there. But everything else I did BY THE BOOK. If the teacher's manual told me to review with flashcards 21–49, then you can be sure that I didn't use 20–50. I might mess things up! We did every single workbook page and other form of drill, even if Ben had already mastered the concept. I was afraid to rock the boat. He did receive an excellent foundation, and thankfully for both of us, his learning style fit right in with my teaching style, which fit right in with the curriculum we chose.

Chapter Three

A Fresh Wind Blows

After several years of these curricula, several years of attendance at homeschool conferences, and reading countless books about how kids learn, we grew dissatisfied with our plan, which actually wasn't much of a plan. Looking back, we realized we had not evaluated it up until then. One thing I did know was that if I had to listen to more children (Luke was getting ready to begin school) reading from mind-numbingly boring readers, someone was going to get hurt. When Ben would read aloud from those books, I would doze off – hardly a picture of a perfect homeschool mom!

> *It's not a question of whether it's a good curriculum. It's a question of whether it's a good choice for your student and your family.*

Then we happened on an old book by Diane Lopez called Teaching Children. This book opened my eyes to what appealed to me about schooling my kids at home. I couldn't articulate it, but she did. From her, I learned that it was possible to use something other than a textbook approach and that we could have the kids learn together in a more relaxed atmosphere. That year, we took steps to introduce a less familiar format to our homeschool. It was still structured, but it was more interesting! We were also gaining a better idea of the family we wanted to create through this process.

After a few more years of experience, a few more conferences attended, and a few more books read, we stretched our wings further to adopt an eclectic approach using lots of *real* books rather than textbooks. I had begun to feel more secure choosing what I felt was best for my family, rather than what everyone else was using. Chris offered his valuable male perspective to my choices, which were usually more girl-centric than boy- friendly, and we adapted and changed curriculum as best suited each child. This involved major stretching on my part.

I'd rather curl up on the couch with my nose in a book and read. I finished my schooling by reading and filling out a nifty worksheet that required that I answer ridiculously simple fill-in-the-blank questions. I'd memorize it all for the test and promptly do a cranial dump to make room for the next batch of information. This earned me good grades in school! But I'm not sure how much I actually learned. Our curriculum choices to fit the boys pushed me out of my box – far out of my box.

I remember once talking to a friend who counseled me about needed changes in our homeschool. I told her that I didn't want to get my house messy with projects. "Bev," she chided, "you're such a wimp!" I believe those were her exact words, and I am grateful for her honesty. I still struggle with mustering the motivation to engage in a project involving raw whole chickens, but it isn't about me, is it?

That said, I learned to buck the system even with that particular curriculum, and I did not complete every recommended activity. So there! Can you imagine the audacity of not following the suggested plan or letting a few worksheets go blank? I learned to balance my teaching style and my children's learning styles, and to follow their lead. That was hard for me. I'm boring, but I'm learning to adapt. I'm learning that it's easy to get caught up in the method of homeschooling and forget that it's simply a means to an end. The education of my children is the end, and the path taken is of secondary importance. I want great adults as the end product of our homeschool, and it won't be the curriculum that I choose that determines that. That bears repeating. The curriculum choices that I make do not guarantee me anything. Children are people, not products.

This is especially important to recognize now. The demand for homeschool curricula has exploded, and with it has come some exciting options that offer families a lot of variety from which to choose. That's a good thing – as long as we're actually choosing based on our unique family makeup and not based on what everyone else is doing. Know this, methods and popular curriculum choices in homeschool circles come in and out of fashion. Let's face it. We can feel pressure to use the latest thing that everyone else is using because it must be good if everyone is using it. I know I did! It's not a question of whether it's a good curriculum. It's a question of whether it's a good choice for your student and your family. Determining the answer to that requires some thoughtful examination, and we'll get to that.

Chapter Four

TAKE INVENTORY

Charting a course for your homeschool by any other map than the one that God has provided for your family is a recipe for stress, strained relationships, broken dreams, lack of joy, and burnout. Do you know what that map is, or are you just doing what everyone else is doing? Are you brave enough to follow God's leading? I'm assuming that most of us are in this homeschool thing for the long haul. If we want to finish the race set before us, we must "lay aside every encumbrance, and the sin which so easily entangles us, and let us run with endurance the race that it set before us, fixing our eyes on Jesus, the author and perfecter of faith, who for the joy set before Him endured the cross, despising the shame, and has sat down at the right hand of the throne of God." Heb. 12:1 – 2. New American Standard Bible.

Make no mistake; accepting the responsibility of educating your own kids is a choice that will require endurance on your part! We do well to prepare ourselves to have staying power, so don't set yourself up for failure. Here are some things that might encumber or entangle us and wear us out: separate soccer teams

TAKE INVENTORY

for each child in our family, foreign language lessons for our elementary age children, serving in multiple areas/roles in our church home, serving in multiple volunteer capacities in each of our children's activities, swim lessons, baseball teams, AWANA, boy scouts, choir, band, youth group, babysitting, Moms' night out, or support groups. Then there's the ever popular entanglement of comparing ourselves to others – their homes, their children's academic prowess, their extra activities, their church involvement, their perfect good looks....

I want my adult children to homeschool their children because they view their years at home as something worth emulating. If our homeschool consists of power charged hours spent in the car rushing frantically from one activity to another, are they going to want to duplicate that with my grandchildren? Do you ever arrive at these activities in a state of peace and joy? Aren't we more often than not frazzled and irritated? I want my grown kids to look back on our homeschool days with fondness.

I'm not suggesting that the above-mentioned activities are bad. However, we do need to honestly evaluate if each of these activities is appropriate for our particular season in life. Are they suitable for the makeup of our family, for the goals we have set forth for our family, and most importantly, do they move us closer to our goal? Recall the principle from 1 Cor. 6:12, "All things are good but not all things are profitable." Do we just blow it at the "all" part – trying to do it all, all the time, as opposed to determining to choose what is best? I've heard it said, "You can have it all, just not all at the same time." I submit that there is truth to that. What someone else's family needs isn't necessarily what your family needs.

> **_The goal is to maximize effectiveness and simplicity because if whatever we're doing lacks either of those qualities, we won't do it for very long._**

Periodically, we need to re-evaluate what we're doing! We start off in a direction and neglect to re-evaluate our course as life changes. What was valuable to us when we started may no longer be beneficial, and we may need to say "No, not now" to certain activities. Perhaps we can come back to them later on, perhaps not. Ladies, if your husband is good at reining in your tendency to overdo, don't thwart his efforts to rein you in. Be grateful that God put him there to lead your family, and don't continue on in your own stubborn way! If you ignore his advice, you will reap the consequences of your choices. What kind of consequences? I suggest that they are stress, illness, anxiety, despair, and lack of joy. Sadly, everyone in the family will be affected.

The point is to determine if what we're doing at this moment is right for what we're trying to accomplish. The goal is to maximize effectiveness and simplicity because if whatever we're doing lacks either of those qualities, we won't do it for very long. Depending on the number of kids you have and the span between their ages, you might have a long future in homeschooling ahead of you. You're going to want to get this right, which means making sure you don't set yourself up for burnout!

Chapter Five

GET A PLAN

I suggest you and your spouse create a set of *living* goals for your family. I use the term 'living' because they may change with changing seasons of life. Some folks call them short-term and long-term goals. Call them what you will, but sit down and commit to paper what it is that you are trying to accomplish with your family. Begin at the end, and work your way backward.

Just what kind of young men and women are you trying to rear? You and I need to contemplate that end product. Then we need to tailor our plans to accomplish that goal. Do I want my children to think that they need to participate in every activity in life, or that they need to carefully choose and commit to a few things and do them well? Do I want my children to believe that we can only learn from experts, or do I want them to understand that with focused effort, there are a lot of things that they can master on their own?

Zoom out for a broader view, and decide what it is you are trying to create. Yes, in your family you are creating something. Is it a lifelong bond between family members where they love, honor, and support one another? Is it young boys and girls who grow into influential men and women for Christ? Is it a place where individuals can find their unique gifts and talents and hone them to excellence? Are you trying to create a place where your children learn the personal self-discipline to pursue their own goals in life? The myriad of choices that we make for our families in our homeschool adventure send messages to our children about what we value. They also affect the outcome. It's going to take time to create these goals. It was a few years before Chris and I figured out what we wanted for our family and our homeschool. Just for fun, below is a copy of our original goals, typos and all.

We have to learn to do what brings the results we desire and stop doing things that simply take up time. This might involve change on our part, and change can be a difficult thing, especially when it involves something that gives us security. We feel secure completing every exercise in the workbook, following the teacher's guide without question, or enrolling our children in classes that others rave about. We need to learn to find our security in knowing that we're making choices based on what is best for our own family, even when it looks different from what everyone else is doing.

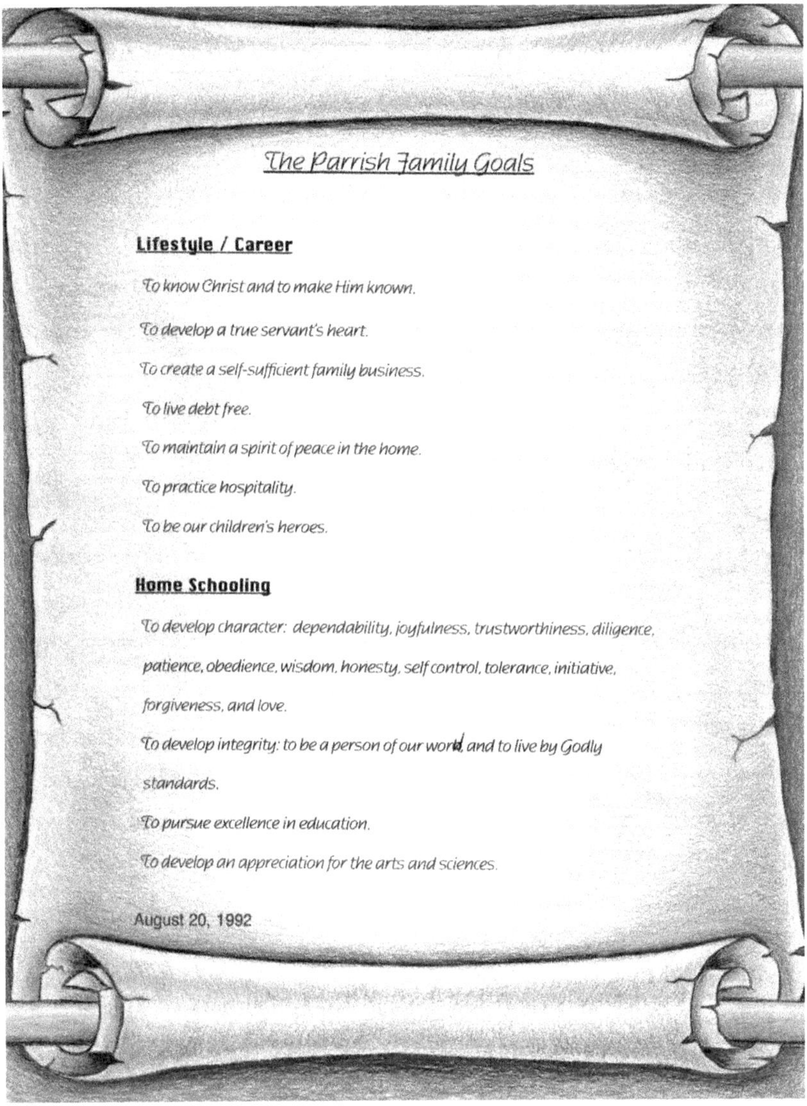

The Parrish Family Goals

Lifestyle / Career

To know Christ and to make Him known.

To develop a true servant's heart.

To create a self-sufficient family business.

To live debt free.

To maintain a spirit of peace in the home.

To practice hospitality.

To be our children's heroes.

Home Schooling

To develop character: dependability, joyfulness, trustworthiness, diligence, patience, obedience, wisdom, honesty, self control, tolerance, initiative, forgiveness, and love.

To develop integrity: to be a person of our word, and to live by Godly standards.

To pursue excellence in education.

To develop an appreciation for the arts and sciences.

August 20, 1992

GET A PLAN

God can enlarge our abilities and strengthen our weaknesses, if we are willing to lay aside what we feel defines us – our personalities, limitations, learning styles, etc. Let me explain. In my case, I have a seriously underdeveloped "fun gene," to coin a friend's phrase. I've told you that I prefer to read books rather than actually *do* things that get me dirty or make a mess. I'm a homebody, and I'm okay with just the company of my family. I can cling to my way, or I can pursue God as he stretches me out of my comfort zone. My children benefit when I follow God into an area where I'm not comfortable. They learn by watching mom learn that the unknown isn't quite so scary after all.

They saw this played out in a big way when I decided that my book knowledge of sailing was insufficient. My family is made up of competent, competitive sailors, except for Hannah and me. The two of us prefer to be deck fluff. However, several years ago it became evident that it was no longer safe for me to be an unskilled passenger on our boat. The older boys were leaving home, and the younger ones weren't competent yet. That meant that if anything should happen to Chris, I would need to know how to handle the boat!

Much to my discomfort, I grudgingly enrolled in a week long, overnight sailing camp for ladies. Note two things here: camp and overnight. I don't like either. Full disclosure though, we weren't camping exactly. We were staying in a hotel, but I use that term loosely. I like my bed, my bed partner, and my routine. Here I found myself with lots of women I did not know, most of whom knew each other (yuck), sleeping in a lumpy bed with a loud roomie. However, the instruction was wonderful, and at the end of the week, my family sailed our boat over to the sheltered cove where we were learning, dropped anchor, and watched me demonstrate my new skills. They were pretty proud. I was, too. Granted, sailing hardly has eternal consequences, but God uses the mundane things of our everyday lives to cause us to grow. I gained confidence, and not just in sailing. My kids saw that.

> ## *The family is an excellent proving ground that molds its members into the image of Christ*

I have the choice of insisting on my way, or being flexible and taking the chance that I just might enjoy a change. I encourage my children to extend themselves and try something that they don't feel comfortable trying. Why wouldn't I do the same? I'm being a hypocrite if I don't.

Could it be that God has us on this journey of homeschooling—in addition to the academics—primarily because the family is an excellent proving ground that molds its members into the image of Christ? Could it be that when you and I resist changing ourselves, we thwart the very thing that would be used to make us into who we're supposed to be? Could it be that when we choose things because there is comfort in following others, we miss out on the benefits we'd get if we did what was designed for our family? Following someone else's path won't lead us to *our* destination. We are not called to fit in with the crowd.

GET A PLAN

Once while working out at the gym, a young woman asked me about an exercise I was doing and what body part it was working. She told me how frustrated she was with her weight training. She'd been training for six years or so, and hadn't seen the results she wanted. We talked about the importance of good form in achieving your exercise goals. I showed her how to do a few exercises using correct form, and had her choose a lighter weight. Her surprised response was, "Wow! I can feel *that*!"

There is a principle here that we can apply to our homeschooling. Longtime weight trainers will tell you that it isn't *just* the amount of weight that you lift that creates a strong, well-balanced body. Proper form and focus are both essential. In fact, it is possible to use lighter weights, concentrate on proper form, and get excellent results. We can do this only when the load we are lifting is not so heavy that it causes us to compensate and use momentum to perform the exercise. Simply lifting heavy weights without correct form or intention won't produce the body you want. It will likely get you hurt. Focused, specific exercises, correctly done, will achieve what you desire.

The takeaway from this is that all these frenetic activities in our lives aren't necessarily going to combine to give us our goal. Maybe we have filled our schedules with so many activities that we have to cheat and just go through the motions rather than gain the benefit that is only possible through focusing on a few things and doing them well. We're afforded one go-round in this life, and it's worth it to slow down enough to enjoy.

Let's set goals for our family, just like goals for work or saving for a new car. Shame on us if we spend more time planning how we're going to get out of debt than we do determining what it is that we want our families to become! Before we go on a trip, we need to know where we're going. If we're homeschooling, we're going on a trip! How much serious thought have we put into what we want to accomplish in homeschooling our kids? What is the end result we're looking for? If you haven't given it any thought, you need to. Ask God. He promises to give us wisdom. Trust in his wisdom and stop looking at what others are doing. As you do this, bear in mind that one day your children will leave your home as men and women. What kind of adults do you want them to be?

Here are questions you might want to consider:
— What do I want my children to know and value?
— What worldview do I want to pass along?
— What is our family DNA?
— What's important to us? Being physically active and healthy? Being politically active? Serving others?
— Is college a must?
— Do we want our children to be skilled in a trade?
— Is it important to us that they study something that we believe will provide a secure job?
— Do we want them to have exceptional relational skills?
— Are we looking to develop confident, self-directed, curious life-long learners?
— When we're finished, will our kids be prepared for anything other than one more year of school?

If we have a Biblical worldview, I hope that we answer those questions in line with Biblical principles and not according to cultural standards. Families are God's domain. Let's not impose man's ideas about achievement on God's domain. There is a myth that long-term success in life is entirely about academic performance. That is a lie! Ask business owners, and they will tell you that they desperately need hard working, self-motivated, responsible employees who are willing and able to be trained.

Additionally, in *How Children Succeed,* author Paul Tough points to studies that indicate it is actually the qualities of good character that have a greater impact than academic prowess on our future success as adults. We need to rethink the conventional wisdom that academics and college is a guarantee of success.

"What is my greatest hope for my kids when they leave my home?"

I ask you again, how much serious thought have you put into what you want to accomplish in homeschooling your kids? We must know our goals before we can wisely choose curriculum or methods. Those choices can have a huge effect on our family life, so we should compare them against our goals. There are limited hours in the day, and our choices either free up or use up that time. That's important to know.

Another wonderful question to contemplate is "What is my greatest hope for my kids when they leave my home?" Stop and ponder that one for a moment. Go ahead, I'll wait. Dream big things for your kids. I'm not talking about big houses, big paychecks, or big titles. I'm talking about dreaming big that they will live lives and have relationships that positively influence their culture. For some, that influence will come from faithfully tending to their little corner of the world, raising disciples who love and serve God and their fellow man. For others, it may come in more visible ways.

Dream bigger than an impressive SAT score and college degree. Dream bigger than impressive cars and houses. Your children are more than merely students. They are unique and created in the image of a wonderful God who has a plan for their *whole* life – spiritually, mentally, academically, physically, relationally. Remember to take the time necessary to develop these ideas. Dream dreams of substance for your kids. Dream of what they will become rather than what they will acquire. Dream dreams worthy of their Creator's plans.

Chapter Six

ADJUST YOUR EXPECTATIONS

Now that you've decided to homeschool, you can count on big changes in your life. You'll need a whole new set of expectations! There will be a period of adjustment when things don't work just right. Maybe you used to work outside the home. You're not just beginning homeschooling, you're changing your lifestyle. Even if you have always been home with your kids, educating them changes things. If they were in a typical school setting (public or private), you were probably accustomed to choosing how to spend your day. Things you used to do might have to go, either permanently or maybe just for a while. You're now a mom with an additional full-time job. Give everyone time to get used to the new normal. View this time with your kids as a great blessing. You have the distinct privilege of influencing them all day! You've probably heard this expression, "We teach what we know. We reproduce what we are." Our kids are watching us. That should make us fall on our knees each morning to seek God's wisdom and the transforming power of the Holy Spirit!

All of you will need to acquire new habits. Homeschooling isn't rocket science, and it's quite efficient. It doesn't have to take

ADJUST YOUR EXPECTATIONS

up all of your time, but it will require a different mindset to get it accomplished. If your kids are very young and you're just beginning their education, much of it is going to be centered around everyday life; that's not too complicated. If you have multiple ages of kids who you will be educating, it requires a bit more purposeful planning of your time. You don't need to be rigid. Neither do you want to act in a sloppy manner.

Remember that when you begin to homeschool, or any time life changes in a big way (like a new baby or a new student added to the mix), you all need time to adapt. And what we're doing isn't merely school at home. *It's a new way of living.* An important step toward long-term success in this venture is to simplify your life. I'm talking about possessions, commitments, and expectations. Everything you own costs you time to maintain. Ask yourself if it's worth it, and get rid of it if it isn't. Be sure you're tending to things you value. Declutter your world as best you can. Commitments require emotional energy, so you might need to reconsider things you committed to before you began homeschooling. Know yourself and your family, and honestly assess your situation. Are your days filled with more activities than you can possibly accomplish? Are they moving you toward your family goals? Realistically evaluating your expectations about what life is supposed to be like is extremely freeing! Let go of the idea that every moment must be a memorable experience worthy of sharing on social media. It's impossible to sustain that image.

Chapter Seven

SET YOURSELF UP FOR SUCCESS

> *Keep everything as simple as possible.*
> *You want your focus to be on the stuff*
> *that matters*

In the beginning, if your budget allows, it might be helpful to have housekeeping help, grocery delivery, or dry cleaning pickup. Hire a teenager to run errands for you. It's not set in stone forever. Your family needs to learn to care for the household they're living in, but you might need to work up to getting it all done. If your children are quite young, you don't have a lot of helpers for household chores, so it's not unreasonable to ask for help. Extend grace to yourself! There have been many years in our married lives when we couldn't afford any extra expense associated with convenience, so we just tried to keep everything as simple as possible. You want your focus to be on the stuff that matters, rather than trying to do it all yourself.

Let me throw in a freebie here. You might even consider a uniform for you and the kids just to keep things simple and eliminate unnecessary decisions! Thankfully, our kids have always had simple wardrobes by choice. They've been content with jeans or shorts and t-shirts – usually just a few that they enjoyed over and over, sort of a uniform. For several years, I had a uniform as well – jeans and a white or a black tee. It was a wonderful no-brainer in the morning. I felt reasonably put together, and it required very little effort. I don't do it anymore, but while I did, it was liberating. I strongly suggest that you at least establish a firm one-outfit-per-day-unless-there-are-bodily-fluids-involved policy. That goes for kids and parents.

It's important to have an accurate perspective about the time necessary to properly educate your children. Remember that what we do as homeschoolers is much more efficient than a conventional school setting, so it doesn't take as long. You might be counting your children, doing the math, and deciding that there's no way you can possibly educate multiple kids and get it all done. The easiest option is combining subjects to maximize your time. It's a good family bonding time, as well, to read aloud and study subjects together. Those that lend themselves easily to combining multiple ages are history, literature, science, and Bible. Even if you are using a textbook-centered curriculum, you could still combine kids and read aloud from the textbook. Target the middle to the oldest age, and everyone learns.

Bear this time guideline in mind to keep from overwhelming yourself or your young kids. Unless your state law specifies otherwise, it is not necessary to follow a typical school schedule of required hours of instruction. Think for a moment about just the core subjects of language, arts and math. For a kindergartner, a combined total of about one-half hour of *one-on-one direct instruction* is sufficient. Depending on the child, you might need to break up even this short amount of time. Thereafter, add one-half hour for each grade. A first grader would have a maximum of one hour of *direct one-on-one instruction*; a third grader would have two hours; etc. The guideline is primarily intended to remind you that it is unnecessarily cumbersome to have a five-year-old doing three or more hours of direct instruction of school each day! After this one-on-one instruction in the core subjects of math and language arts, add in the others your children are studying. Don't get stuck on trying to figure out exactly how much time to spend for each grade in later years, because when our students get older, the guideline isn't as accurate. I mention it to protect your little ones from too much work!

Some school days will be longer than others. Some co-ops are all day long and meet multiple times a week. I'm not talking about those instances. I'm talking about what *characterizes* your homeschool day. I realize that this seems like such a small amount of time, and it is. The one-on-one tutorial nature of homeschooling is intense and highly efficient compared to a classroom environment with lots of kids where a classroom teacher has much more to accomplish than just teaching. You're right there, recognizing when your child understands and is ready to move on, or needs further instruction. Depending on the size of your family, your attention is on fewer students as well. Don't use time spent in institutional school settings as a measure of how much time will be needed in your homeschool. You're going to cover a lot more material in a shorter period of time.

Even with appropriate expectations for your kids' instruction time, if you still feel overwhelmed, consider staggering when you begin each child's school year. Start one child the first week in September, get them up and going with a routine, and add another child the second week. Additionally, you could stagger the start times of various subjects and ease yourself and your family into a full schedule gradually. Begin with two subjects the first week, and add in additional subjects as you get your feet under you. This gentle approach reassures you that you will in fact survive! When you've accomplished enough school to reach the first holiday (yeah!), remember this guideline when it's time to return to studies: give yourself one day of ramping up for every week you had off. That doesn't mean you don't do any school during that time, it just means that you recognize everyone got out of the habit of expecting to study. You might have to woo your students, and yourself, back into the groove! Remember this is a journey, not a race. I suggest these guidelines to help you to adjust your thinking and prevent you from trying to exactly duplicate school at home.

Chapter Eight

Taming Your Schedule

You need to be aware of your habits and actions relating to the use of your time. Whether you like it or not, you are the model for your children. If you did not grow up learning principles of organization and prioritization, you may lack such basic skills yourself. Maybe you grew up with an ultra-organized, well-prioritized life, but your parents imposed that on you rather than taught you the principles. Whatever the case, you can learn along with your family while you're in the process of implementing some simple principles. Understand that managing and prioritizing time is about managing yourself. This might mean that you need to explore a few new habits. We have as much time as we have, and we all have the exact same 1,440 minutes per day. Managing time is about the choices we make. When we choose to invest time in an activity, by default, we choose not to do something else, and we can't do everything! To choose wisely, you must know yourself and your family. This is another place where your family goals come in to give you direction. Remind yourself what is valuable to you. What do you make time for every day? What would you do if you had one more hour each day? If you had one less hour, what would you cut out? You want to acquire the mindset of evaluating commitments rather than mindlessly adding them to your life. In order to effectively evaluate, you need to know the truth about your situation. We'll cover the three steps in this chapter and the next.

Step One is determining the truth about your yearly schedule. I recommend printing out a large linear calendar that shows an entire year in one long strip. The site www.studenthandouts.com has nice ones. They look similar to this one I created:

JAN	FEB	MARCH	APRIL	MAY	JUNE	JULY	AUG	SEP	OCT	NOV	DEC
1	1	1	1	1	1	1	1	1	1	1	1
2	2	2	2	2	2	2	2	2	2	2	2
3	3	3	3	3	3	3	3	3	3	3	3
4	4	4	4	4	4	4	4	4	4	4	4
5	5	5	5	5	5	5	5	5	5	5	5
6	6	6	6	6	6	6	6	6	6	6	6
7	7	7	7	7	7	7	7	7	7	7	7
8	8	8	8	8	8	8	8	8	8	8	8
9	9	9	9	9	9	9	9	9	9	9	9
10	10	10	10	10	10	10	10	10	10	10	10
11	11	11	11	11	11	11	11	11	11	11	11
12	12	12	12	12	12	12	12	12	12	12	12
13	13	13	13	13	13	13	13	13	13	13	13
14	14	14	14	14	14	14	14	14	14	14	14
15	15	15	15	15	15	15	15	15	15	15	15
16	16	16	16	16	16	16	16	16	16	16	16
17	17	17	17	17	17	17	17	17	17	17	17
18	18	18	18	18	18	18	18	18	18	18	18
19	19	19	19	19	19	19	19	19	19	19	19
20	20	20	20	20	20	20	20	20	20	20	20
21	21	21	21	21	21	21	21	21	21	21	21
22	22	22	22	22	22	22	22	22	22	22	22
23	23	23	23	23	23	23	23	23	23	23	23
24	24	24	24	24	24	24	24	24	24	24	24
25	25	25	25	25	25	25	25	25	25	25	25
26	26	26	26	26	26	26	26	26	26	26	26
27	27	27	27	27	27	27	27	27	27	27	27
28	28	28	28	28	28	28	28	28	28	28	28
29		29	29	29	29	29	29	29	29	29	29
30		30	30	30	30	30	30	30	30	30	30
31		31		31		31	31		31		31

If you want to go for visual shock and awe, try cutting apart a monthly paper calendar and taping the pages together in one long view. It sounds archaic, but for this particular step, you need the sobering visual of your year laid out before you. It's much more impactful than anything on a screen. Record every single activity you know you will be doing during the school year and see the full scope at one time. Include church, co-op, lessons, sports, monthly meetings, and vacations. If you're exhausted after this part of the exercise, that's a red flag! The beauty of a large paper version is that everyone can see everything at one time. This is important for several reasons. If you are just using your phone or other electronic calendar, it's quite possible that you're seeing only short stretches of the year at a time. You want to be able to see the entire school year. It will be the reality check that helps you determine if an activity needs to go, or if you've got margin to add in things in which you would like to participate. This is a wonderful opportunity to begin teaching your children about prioritizing commitments, and paper lends itself to more easily showing them the big picture. Once you've done the preliminary work of assessing your present schedule, go back to your preferred method if you like.

Step two is to get a closer view. This is where you're going see an hour by hour view of what your family does each day. Check out www.studenthandouts.com again, to print out a one-week version that has an hourly listing down one side, or make your own using my example here:

TAMING YOUR SCHEDULE

Hours	Monday	Tuesday	Wednesday	Thursday	Friday	Saturday	Sunday
6:00 a.m.							
6:30 a.m.							
7:00 a.m.							
7:30 a.m.							
8:00 a.m.							
8:30 a.m.							
9:00 a.m.							
9:30 a.m.							
10:00 a.m.							
10:30 a.m.							
11:00 a.m.							
11:30 a.m.							
Noon							
12:30 p.m.							
1:00 p.m.							
1:30 p.m.							
2:00 p.m.							
2:30 p.m.							
3:00 p.m.							
3:30 p.m.							
4:00 p.m.							
4:30 p.m.							
5:00 p.m.							
5:30 p.m.							
6:00 p.m.							
6:30 p.m							
7:00 p.m.							
7:30 p.m.							
8:00 p.m.							
8:30 p.m.							
9:00 p.m.							
9:30 p.m.							
10:00 p.m.							
10:30 p.m.							
11:00 p.m.							

    Block out the hours of ongoing activities in your days. Don't forget to count time spent corralling kids into clean clothing, gathering necessary items, and travel both ways. Include meals and preparation time, bedtime rituals, naps, everything. If you're feeling brave, make note of time spent on electronic devices, and I'm talking about you, not your kids. Now you have a more thorough picture of what your daily life looks like.

    Honestly assess where you are compared to where you want to be, and be bold enough to make decisions that keep you in line with your family goals. Decide to stop doing those things that merely consume your time rather than enhance your life. I propose that for some of you posting on social media is consuming vast amounts of your time. When I sit down to check mine, I am shocked at the frequency with which some of my homeschool mom friends are posting and wonder how they even interact with their children. I hope you have the courage to honestly measure its worth to you. You cannot get back the time lost with your attention on a screen.

When you fine-tune your days to focus on the things you truly value, you'll find peace seeping back into your life. You might meet resistance from friends and family. Be careful not to let others determine the best use of your time. For example, the co-op that everyone is participating in and the extracurricular activity that your child needs or she "won't be a well-rounded student" are subject to scrutiny! Be ruthless, and jealously guard your days; you can always add in activities later. Starting small and adding things in is much better than having to eliminate things to which you have already committed.

Chapter Nine

BUT WHAT DO I DO MONDAY?

Now we're ready for Step Three, which I like to think of as *ordering* your time – assigning the proper priority to what is to be done, rather than what might be screaming for your attention. There are two main priorities in your homeschool day: running your home/tending to your family, and educating your kids. Don't forget it's vital to establish from the beginning what your ultimate goals are because having goals creates boundaries and guides your decisions. There are numerous ways to schedule your homeschool day, and no one way is better than another. You'll want to experiment to determine what works best for you.

One option is to dedicate blocks of time to do certain things. For instance, you could set aside 9 a.m. to noon for school. I've seen families even successfully require that everyone stay in or near the school room/area during that time. They would take breaks, but unless it was a bathroom break, they remained in the area. It kept everyone focused. It is critical to guard that time slot from things that sabotage it, like a dentist appointment that's only available this Wednesday at 10:00. Really? There is nothing available on other days later in the afternoon? Having a dedicated school time leaves the rest of the day to be spent on appointments, extracurricular activities, play dates, etc. We did this for a while and found it very motivating for everyone. We all knew we had to work hard for that time frame, and then the rest of the day was free. A variation of this would be to assign subjects to blocks of time. For example, everyone does language arts from 9:00 to 9:45, and math from 10:00 to 10:45. You get the picture. Doing this allows you as the teacher to get your brain in math mode and deal with any and all math questions in one sitting. Any manipulatives or other supplies are all out and accessible. When math time is done, everything is put away and you have a clean table to tackle the next subject.

Another possibility might be scheduling an hour at a time. No matter when you get up, the first hour is for getting ready for the day, the second hour is reading aloud/Bible, the third hour is independent work, and on it goes. This might work well for a family with a new baby or other circumstance that necessitates flexibility. It also provides helpful structure. Some families prefer having an appointment with each child for a specified time. During the first hour of the school day, you work with Kiddo A, the second hour is time for Kiddo B, the third hour belongs to Kiddo C, etc. This way everyone knows they have a dedicated time with you, and it helps them learn to show consideration for each other's school needs. Instruct kids beforehand on what to do if they need you before their designated time. Often they will have figured out their problem on their own while they wait! Using this plan can increase your children's self-reliance, initiative, and responsibility. It gives them an opportunity to practice those skills while knowing that you'll be checking in with them soon. Take these suggestions as a starting point, and give yourself permission to mix and match. Change as needed. The take away is that you are the boss here, and you are only limited by your imagination in how to order your school day.

Keeping a few principles in mind can be helpful to stack the deck in your favor for success. Don't check your email, social media, or make phone calls first thing in the morning. This is a recipe for distraction and entering your school day in an agitated state of mind. Maybe it's just me, but there's nothing like a frustrating phone call with a customer service department to set me directly on the path to the bad place first thing in the morning. I can let that derail my attitude for the whole day. Let's be honest, few of us are in such demand that we need to respond instantly to every chirp, beep, or buzz. Set a designated time when you plan to check on those things and stick to it. Turn off the notifications on your phone; you'll be a good example to your kids!

An additional principle to keep in mind is to decide each day on the top three things you want to accomplish. Write them down and indicate how you will reward yourself for completing each one. The reward could be a cup of coffee, ten minutes on social media, ten minutes alone reading. The choice is yours. You will find that numerous distractions in the form of *opportunities* will present themselves throughout the day. In order to maintain focus on your family's priorities, a vital skill to master is how to say "No." You may even need to tell yourself "No." Let's practice. Repeat after me, "No." Try again. "No." See, that's not hard. If you're not certain whether you want to participate in the proposed opportunity, it helps if you learn to respond graciously with, "That sounds interesting. Let me check with my spouse and our schedule before I answer," or "Let me get back to you on that." You might want to practice those as well! Never agree to a commitment, no matter how noble, without checking in with your family's schedule and long-term goals. If you maintain boundaries for yourself and your family in the beginning, you are more likely to homeschool long term without unnecessary stress.

If time management isn't your strength, allow yourself the freedom to explore different things to find a good fit. The idea is to implement habits that make your world run more efficiently and smoothly. The time police aren't going to show up at your house and grade you on how well you are implementing a plan. Expect a period of trial and error. Give yourself grace to fail, dust yourself off, and try something different.

Chapter Ten

SURVIVAL SKILLS FOR THE REAL WORLD – AKA CHORES

Let's talk briefly about chores because they affect your time and how you prioritize it. Get everyone involved, and put it on the schedule. View it as an appointment that all family members are expected to attend. If you've been doing everything for your family until now, this homeschool adventure is a prime opportunity to teach self-reliance. Maybe you want a family goal to be to raise responsible, self-reliant men and women who aren't at a loss if mom goes out of town. Getting your family or yourself, if you are challenged in this area, on board with maintaining your home is going to require extra effort in the beginning. If you are adept at keeping the household running, you're going to be tempted to continue to do everything yourself because it's so much faster (and it gets done like you like it, which is of course the *right* way, but we won't go there). You'd be right; it is faster to do it yourself, in the short term. You have to think long term. You can teach your family members to do most everything! This isn't a hard and fast principle for all seasons of life, however.

While I'm a huge fan of including even the littlest ones in household maintenance, understand that sometimes you just need to get a chore done. Alone. Forgo the teaching moment and unload the dishwasher yourself. If allowing your youngest kids to help with every chore means that you are constantly behind, it's okay to limit their help occasionally. You won't be sentencing them to a lifetime of helplessness or permanent residency in your guest room. We've found it helpful to assign chores for a year at a time. That allows everyone the opportunity to develop a reliable habit of doing them, as well as achieve mastery. There's an end date, albeit a long way off, if it's a chore they dislike. In my opinion, when you're in charge of some area of maintenance for a while, you begin to own it. My kids developed the habit of policing one another to be sure no one was carelessly messing up the work they had done. This meant that overall my kids were becoming more careful about the messes they created.

If this doesn't sound very fun to you and you'd rather adopt a system with cool rewards for work well done, bear in mind that I'm suggesting this as a means of paving the way for success. Be fun if you want to be fun, but first I'd recommend getting everyone in the habit of doing the chores. Otherwise, you've created another job for yourself with this system of keeping track of all the fun everyone is having. The truth of the matter is that life is full of responsibilities that aren't enjoyable and go unrewarded. Helping to keep the home running is an opportunity to serve one another in love. Don't forget that you are raising men and women who will one day be on their own, and they'll need to know how to care for themselves and their families.

Chapter Eleven

Choosing Curriculum that Fits

If home education gives us the opportunity to choose or design a curriculum that allows our children to be who they are supposed to be, why would we simply follow the crowd? Perhaps we feel pressure from family to proceed in a way that is similar to the school environment that they knew. Maybe we feel unspoken pressure from our friends whose kids are in traditional schools to choose curriculum that appears quite rigorous, so we can prove that homeschooled kids receive a superior education. It could even be that we are influenced by our homeschooling friends to choose a method they have chosen so we'll be together in co-op!

The truth is that we need to give ourselves the grace to make mistakes!

In order to make good choices for our family, we need to recognize that popular methods and curriculum come and go. When we're new to the homeschooling landscape and we discover that everyone seems to be using a particular method or curriculum, it's easy to assume that it's the best option. It might be for some families, but it might not be for yours. The sheer magnitude of choices is overwhelming, and we might choose a curriculum just to stop the noise in our heads! The truth is that we need to give ourselves the grace to make mistakes. We also need to have the courage to honestly evaluate our motivations for making a particular choice, and if we choose poorly, have the courage to adapt or change. If adapting isn't an option and things aren't working, it's okay to stop using it!

Our goal should be finding the right fit. It may not be perfect, but we can find something that creates an environment where our children can learn with ease. Consider this. You can probably write your name with either your dominant or non-dominant hand. But which one is the most efficient? Which one demonstrates your true handwriting ability? Which one is the easiest? As such, our curriculum and methodology choices should be full of ease. They should also fit the goals we have set for our family and our homeschool.

The curriculum is just a tool we use to accomplish our goals, but we want the one suited to our family. It helps to ask some questions. For example, what do I think is the best way for learning to happen? Do I want my children only around their age mates? Do I want them to have lots of varied real life experiences? Do I want experts to teach? Do I want them to direct their own learning? Do we want to learn together as a family? Am I confident to teach, or willing to learn to teach? Am I a fan of relaxed learning that starts at a later age?

We also need to acknowledge our unique family situation. Does one parent travel for work, or are you a single parent family? In either case, it dramatically affects how much energy and time is available. Do both parents work? Are there complicating health issues? Is there a new baby in the mix? Have we recently moved and aren't settled in yet? Do we have a struggling learner who requires more individual attention and time? Were the kids previously in a public or private school setting? If that's the case, a time of decompression is helpful. A good rule of thumb is to allow one month of decompression for every year they were in school. If you're pulling out a fourth grader, allow four months of decompression time. Now let's define what I mean by decompression time. I don't mean that you plan to plunk them down on the couch with video games and their phone to play with for four months, with no school. I do mean that you adjust your expectations for what your homeschool life will look like for several months. Don't expect to jump right into their studies on day one as if nothing changed.

The life of a child in a typical school setting is vastly different from that at home. Most kids haven't learned to make any decisions for themselves. Everything about their day was scheduled and not necessarily around anything more meaningful than a test. Kids get this. Lots of kids will come home to school having no idea that they can learn on their own, and without a textbook in hand or a teacher standing at the front of the room.

They lack confidence in their own ability to learn by themselves. Contrast this with a child who has been homeschooled from the beginning. Often at the fourth or fifth grade level, they are able to confidently pursue some of their studies on their own, and actually learn!

We need to pay special attention if we're bringing home an older student who has character or relational issues. Resolving relational conflicts and growing good character take time and attention. Creating good character and having a rigorous academic experience aren't mutually exclusive, but if you've got a kiddo with significant issues, it would be wise to find effective ways to deal with that first before embarking on a highly academic course of study. It's okay to go slow. Choosing to focus first on academics out of fear of falling behind will interfere with our attention to the greater issues of character and relationships. Don't plan to use school as a character building opportunity for them. Find other ways to address character issues, so you don't turn them off to what they might be learning. Typically, kids' attention to their work in school can be one of many areas where you see evidence of their character, or lack of it. But this is not necessarily so if there are complicating learning, character, or relational problems. My point is that there are other ways to develop good character without using schoolwork.

My favorite character builders are service to others and hard work. When we serve others, we quickly get a more accurate picture of our self and our life. Areas in which we were certain we were being treated unfairly begin to lose their hold on us when we get up close and personal with someone else's troubles. There is no need to travel far to find a place where someone can benefit from our help. It doesn't require an expensive mission trip out of the country. It can be as uncomplicated as mowing the yard for an elderly neighbor. Likewise, don't discount the value of serving other family members in the course of everyday life. This is as simple as encouraging your child to find a way to help a sibling every day. Actively looking for ways to meet the needs of those around us is a wonderful opportunity to get our attention off us.

That hard work I mentioned can be as mundane as chores around the house that require extra effort, like clearing out the garage, pulling weeds, or cleaning windows. The physical exertion alone helps to rid our bodies of pent up anger or stress. Laboring in ways to which we are unaccustomed is humbling, and often pride is driving poor character. Pride also keeps the focus on us, which is never a healthy thing. Good character requires that we consider others more highly than ourselves. Remember that the actions alone of serving others and hard work do not magically remedy a character problem. It takes attention on our part as parents to address the underlying heart attitudes. Especially if you are resolving relational conflicts as well, get in there with your kids, and work and serve alongside them. Everyone will benefit.

Use the decompression time to reconnect with your children. Deal with behavior and attitude issues before you add in expectations for schoolwork. My hope here is to alert you to the fact that you will need to begin dealing with these personal issues before you can expect to fully jump into challenging academics. Some curriculum and method choices take more time and attention than others do, and you and I, as parents, need to decide which is more important in the moment.

Assessing ourselves, our confidence level, and our personal strengths and weaknesses helps us to recognize a curriculum choice that might be too challenging for us to deliver, when we take into consideration our family dynamics as outlined above. We must also guard against choosing what speaks to us but is likely to miss the mark with our kids. Curriculum choices should fit the kids. We are the adults; we are the ones who must adapt. Honestly assessing how much time we have available to direct our homeschool days is vital. When we choose something that is very parent intensive either in delivery on the front end or checking the work on the back end (or both), we need to realistically have the time to do it.

We should also study our kids and their preferred ways of learning. Are they visual, auditory, or kinesthetic learners? Briefly, the visual learner finds the printed word a good fit and is probably content with books or textbooks alone. The auditory learner enjoys listening to their required studies and might like a media-based delivery method or lots of materials read aloud to them. And the kinesthetic learner needs to interact physically with the material in the form of activities or merely move their bodies in order to learn. These kiddos are likely fans of the activities and diverse nature of unit studies. In what areas do you see their preferences?

We need to be careful to respect how our children learn.

It's easy to ascribe more value to a particular learning style over another. We may feel that those who learn readily from the printed page while seated at a desk are the smart kids, and those who prefer to handle and explore things physically, or move their bodies while learning need medication to remedy that "problem." Neither is true. Check out the resources at the back of the book for suggestions on a more thorough exploration of these learning styles. It might take some time to identify your child's needs. That doesn't mean you have to wait to begin. It just means you need pay attention to them so you can adapt if necessary.

Bear in mind that very young children usually tend to be more kinesthetic learners. Until they are about age eight, you'll need lots of concrete activities and movement to satisfy their need to wiggle. After age eight, you will begin to see their preferences for learning play out in how they interact with their studies. Watch them. Learn about them. Keep in mind what you have learned when making curriculum choices. I sure don't want to put my wiggly fourth grader into a program where she will be required to sit at her desk and complete paperwork or view a computer screen for large portions of her day. Perfectly accommodating a child's learning style doesn't work with every subject. But I'm speaking about what characterizes the curriculum choice we make. Playing to their strengths is the most efficient and enjoyable way for your children to learn. Your time with your kids is limited. Spend it wisely by investing in their strengths.

As your children reach upper elementary/middle school and high school years, pay attention to their natural gifts and interests. Don't let your pride limit you if they seem to be interested in an area for which you don't have much regard! Our curriculum choices should begin to aim our children in the direction of their gifts.

Do we have a kid who seems to thrive in and enjoy the academic realm? Is their interest one that requires a college degree? That is important to note as we plan for and choose their curriculum. Do we have a kid who is taking apart everything in the garage and putting it back together in unconventional ways that are better than the original? An activity-based unit study centered on their interests—or for older students an apprenticeship or trade school—might be wise to pursue instead of a book-centered course of study. What if we have a child who has already begun designing, planning, and remodeling our home, as well as promoting those same skills throughout the neighborhood for hire? If finances allow, help them start a business!

All these things about our kids show us how we can effectively spend our time. Certainly, we comply with our state law and meet the requirements it contains. Beyond that, we have the incredible opportunity to tailor an education to fit our child. This was once reserved for the upper echelon of society. Yet we've been given the chance to do something different and set our kids on a trajectory that will launch them into their world more prepared than a one-size-fits-all course of study. We can tell ourselves that the truly valuable things to focus on are the moneymaker items or where we believe the jobs will be in the future. Currently the prevailing wisdom is that the STEM field is where we need to focus. That plays nicely into thinking that those students who excel in STEM fields are smarter than other students. I might have to disagree that a scientist is inherently smarter than my plumber. It's merely expertise in a different area. Frankly, my plumber's job is probably more secure. I don't see him being outsourced any time soon, and I'm willing to pay him incredible sums of money when my toilet is broken! I'm glad we have diverse opportunities for honorable work in our society. Let's not be snobs and limit our children.

We are the stewards of our children's lives.

How about we allow our children the freedom to be who God created them to be? More importantly, how about we esteem and encourage their various gifts, even if it won't amount to the largest bank account or status? Let's get off the treadmill of fear for our children's future and trust God. How about we seek God's wisdom in directing our children's paths to equip them for His plan, be obedient to what He tells them, and then let Him achieve His good purpose? As we ponder our many options, remember this: people build joyful, meaningful lives on their strengths, not on their weaknesses. Play to your children's strengths. We are the stewards of our children's lives. While we easily recognize our God-given stewardship over finances, talents, and creation, do we recognize that we are charged with the responsibility to be wise stewards of our children's time, talent, and character?

Chapter Twelve

HOW MUCH DOES THIS COST?

Before we make a final decision on a curriculum, let's count the true cost. If it requires participation in an outside activity like a co-op, it can be a wonderful benefit to our children's learning. It comes with a price tag however, and we need to be sure that it's one we're willing to pay. Even after evaluating these things, it may still be the right option and completely worth it. Let's just be honest in evaluating that cost. Consider the time requirement, both for your student and for you as the mom ensuring that the assigned work gets done, or for you if you are required to volunteer in some capacity, or how far you have to drive. Evaluate whether your family budget can handle extra meals out. It happens surprisingly often, either while you're out or when you get home because you missed dinner preparation time.

What about gasoline costs and required supplies? Acknowledge that you'll be abiding by another person's schedule and expectations. This can be a helpful thing for some families and a needless stressor for others. Personally, I always want to count the hassle factor. Let's face it ... getting a bunch of people (little and big ones) out the door, homework and supplies in hand, shoes on, and on time can be a challenge. I want to know that the hassle is worth the benefit! Truth be told, sometimes I found that this wonderful activity that was supposed to make my life so much easier turned out to be a huge pain!

Finally, what about the kids? How does this level of activity affect them? We may enjoy the activity because we are able to visit with other moms, get out of the house, and change out of our yoga pants into something more presentable (positive peer pressure). And we feel it helps us to be accountable. Those are all good things. But if the level of activity is too much for our more introverted kiddos or the academic requirements don't allow for a variety of skill levels, is this too much for our kids? None of these things is inherently right or wrong. We just must evaluate HONESTLY!

Outside activities affect our children in other ways, too. Bear in mind that when we put our children in those activities, they are going to be influenced by the other kids in the group. Sometimes we operate under the false assumption that just because someone homeschools, they share our same values. That's not always the case. We need to keep in mind that if, after the homeschool gymnastics class, our little Johnny has learned some exciting new words or behaviors, we might want to reconsider if little Johnny is mature enough to be exposed to those who might cause him to stumble. Am I spending my children's and my family's time wisely if I have to undo every bad behavior they learn while they were involved in these things? Are these activities truly helping me to achieve my goals?

Once we've come this far in assessing our plan, we then need to compare it with our family goals and ask ourselves if this is the *best* way to achieve them. Is it the simplest way, or is it unnecessarily cumbersome and complicated? As we evaluate, let's be sure that our loyalty is to our children's success, and not to one particular curriculum or method that may appeal to us or our friend. Let's be sure we're not viewing the choice as a guarantee of a particular outcome for our children. The long-term significance of the curriculum we choose has little bearing on the success of our children as adults. It's hard to mess up the education of your children, unless of course you fail to educate your children. What the wrong choice of curriculum *can* do is make everyone's life miserable in the process. It will cost us peace. Choose wisely and change if necessary! Here's a tip ... if tears (yours or your children's) are characterizing your homeschool, it's time for a change!

Chapter Thirteen

WHEN CHANGE IS AFOOT

Just when you think you've got it all figured out for your kids, someone or something throws a wrench in the mix. It's important that we also embrace the fact that what worked for one child might not work for the next one. In a classroom, everyone gets the same thing. No need for that at home. Resist the urge to use curriculum "because we paid a lot for it!" We have to pay attention and be in tune with our kids. Why would you invest yourselves in this venture, and then not take advantage of the freedom to change as necessary?

We used a certain unit study curriculum with Ben in high school, and he liked it. Because it had plenty of activities, it seemed that it would be perfect for Luke, who always enjoyed projects and doing things with his hands. Nonetheless, about midway through the year, we noticed a lack of interest and effort from Luke toward his schoolwork. This wasn't characteristic of him. We sat him down and asked what was wrong. We just knew it couldn't be the curriculum. (Remember, it was perfect for him.) His emotional dam broke, and he told us that he hated the curriculum.

I laugh even now at his response. "I hate it when she (the author of the curriculum) asks me, 'How do you feel about...?' Who cares what I feel about it?" he said. You may have guessed that while Luke was a hands-on learner, he was also not our most chatty. These questions were irritating to him because he couldn't figure out how to respond. Needless to say, we adapted the curriculum to better suit him, and everyone was happier. I wanted him to enjoy it and connect with it like Ben had. I wanted him to want to have these amazing, thought-provoking discussions with us about what he was reading, but it just wasn't his style.

I know, everyone says that the high school years are when our young people are supposed to make a coherent, logical verbal argument for what they believe. Those expectations may be true for some of our kids, but not all of them. And how did Luke turn out? Well, that evening the tension was erased from his face and the relief was obvious. He was able to adjust to our adaptations. We still required that he share an opinion on occasion, and he completed it without further anguish. Truthfully, the stuff that he hated was keeping him from enjoying the rest of the assignments, which were things that he did enjoy. He finished that year well. He went on after high school to serve five years in the Marine Corps. I feel sure that they didn't ask him what he felt about things.

What worked for us during one season of our lives might not be the best choice for a different season. It is not a violation of homeschool rules if for a particular season we need to choose a curriculum we're not thrilled about. In fact, often things in life require us to make a choice that may not be the best in a perfect situation, but is the best for our imperfect situation. We had a season when I was caring for my mom who was ill. I was traveling back and forth to her home, and school was falling by the wayside. Not knowing how long this period would last, we knew that we had to make a change. We began using a curriculum delivered by DVD. It was sound academically, but it wasn't our preferred method. It had other things we didn't like, but at least the kids were able to do school. Then one day they said to me, "Mom, we're learning so much now!" Ugh. That one hurt. What they meant was that what we had been doing (before my mom became ill) wasn't challenging them, and they recognized it! We kept at that DVD school for some time. And let me just say, that it has serious benefits. The teachers always have the lessons prepared. They're always ready to go when it's time to start. They have nifty visual aids and virtual field trips. They're always smiling, and they always look nice. Just sayin'.

Chapter Fourteen

IN PRAISE OF THE ORDINARY

Chris's and my end game desires for our children required a method of education that wasn't typical. That might be the case for you as well. The deck is stacked against us if we follow the way it's always been done for the sole reason that *that's* the way it has always been done. You've heard the saying "If you want something different from what you've always had, you'll have to do something different from what you've always done." I applaud the families who in today's world, using usual modes of education, produce remarkable young men and women. I know a few, so I know it can be done. We chose to do it a different way, one that we believed was better suited for the outcome we had in mind.

Make your decisions based on the vision you have for your family, not what supports your pride.

I look around at my homeschooling mom friends and all too frequently see stress, worry, health problems, despair, and complete lack of joy in the journey. I submit that some of this angst could be the result of letting pride drive their choices. When we first began homeschooling, an older couple gave us two pieces of wise advice. I'll tell you one now, and we'll talk about the other later. The counsel was this: Check your parental pride at the door. Make your decisions based on the vision you have for your family, not what supports your pride. Do not let fear drive your decisions. Those two things, pride and fear, should have no place in our decision-making process. They bring chaos and a frantic pace to our homeschools.

Pride tempts us to put our children in activities that have no true value in their lives at the moment, possibly ever. That robs our young ones of time and freedom to just *be*. Pride entices us to choose things for our children because we feel that it makes us look like we're doing a serious job with this homeschool thing, without regard to what is best for the child.

And then there's fear. Fear wants us to believe that we're not good enough to teach our kids, that if we (instead of an expert) teach them _____ (fill in the blank with the subject of your choice), they won't learn it well, they'll never get into college, they'll never get a good job, and they'll never have a good life. And then we'll look bad. Oops, did I say that out loud? An expert is not necessary to teach our children the skills that will truly help them to succeed in life. It's the parents' job to teach tenacity, honesty, courage, kindness, resourcefulness, commitment, and the list goes on. Those are the things that are key to a successful life, not merely specific skill sets.

I'm not saying that it isn't wise to seek help when we're in over our heads, but we let fear cloud our judgment about when it's *really* time to seek help. We read in 2 Timothy 1:7 (ESV), "[F]or God gave us a spirit not of fear but of power and love and self-control." Do you see that? Not only is fear not from God, but also look at what He gives us instead – power, love, and self-control! I don't know about you, but I can use that in my life! God equips us with just the things we need to successfully navigate this world, and fear isn't one of them.

Furthermore, I don't want to send the message to my children that only experts are qualified to teach us. It's good for all of us to have to dig in deep and at least *try* to learn something ourselves. When it's clear that we need help, get help. While at college, Ben was struggling with calculus. We sent him several variations of the *Calculus for Dummies* type books, and he figured it out. Confidence grows when we conquer a difficult subject on our own. Certainly, time constraints can dictate that we get help fast, but not in most cases. I want my kids to trust their own abilities, and to do that, I need to show them that I trust my own abilities.

Fear is likely to breed discontent with our curriculum choices, too. "If only we were using _____ (fill in the blank with whatever curriculum your perfect friend is successfully using for her perfect kids), then my kids would be brilliant." We all know moms who tell us about their three-year-old who is already reading, or their five-year-old who is learning Spanish. But for most of us, our kids will be average in ability. Even still, the homeschool movement seems to be full of stories of exceptional students. That's because those stories are newsworthy. Our regular, everyday average kids aren't. So it goes with media, even good media. Average doesn't sell. If we're not careful, we can easily begin to fear that we don't measure up. I mean our kids don't measure up. It's easy to decide that we are failing if we're not producing academic superstars. The truth is that some of our kids will be average students. But our children can be extraordinary in different ways. They can be confident lifelong learners, hard workers, men and women of excellent character. That will make them extraordinary by any standard.

Sometimes we make adjustments to our homeschool choices because our kids have different needs and abilities requiring different methods. That's not what I'm talking about. I'm talking about the endless insecurity that rules, oh, say around summer-homeschool-conference time. You know what I mean. I have plenty of wonderful resources already to teach my children for the next year, but, oh, that new one just looks so inviting, and it might be even better than what we're using! What if my children are missing out by not using it? What if they have the dreaded GAP in their education? Horrors! I'd better switch curriculum right now and save them from certain lower SAT scores and a doomed future!

We need to relax and trust our instincts. Really, just relax. Tread carefully before farming out your children to experts. Choose curriculum wisely, and if necessary, put blinders on to keep from being tempted by the newest thing! Keep pride out of the picture and make choices based on what your children truly need, rather than what you think looks best to others. Choose substance over symbolism. Big deal if we're using XYZ curriculum that promises to create the next group of brilliant graduates, if that isn't what God has clearly directed for our family. I can blindly choose an educational path for my children based on someone's promise that *this* is the path that gave us the wonderful men and women of our history, but if it doesn't suit my family, it won't give me that result. It's simply pride dressed up in intellectual snobbery, and it comes accessorized with the handbag of superiority.

Having the guarantee of a great end result is tempting. It's tempting to believe that having the perfect curriculum + activity + volunteer equation is all that is necessary to win at this homeschool thing. However, that is simply not true. Show me where God tells us that He will bless our efforts if they are not in line with His plans. There is no one curriculum or educational method that guarantees a perfect end result. When we cease striving after it and rely on God's direction, we can rest and enjoy the journey.

If we let fear cause us to follow the crowd, we risk missing one of the greatest benefits of personally directing our children's education, and that is *personally directing their education*! If we decide on a curriculum, methodology, or activities for our kids because it appeals to us but it doesn't match our child, we become just like the ordinary school setting, offering them a one-size-fits-all education. Girls, we know that one size does not fit all, don't we? Try that with leggings, if you have any doubts.

Let's recall the pioneer homeschooling families who had few resources and fewer opportunities for their children. Yet somehow, these are the kids who proved that the homeschool environment was academically sound and that it produced competent, mature, well-adjusted adults. I propose it was the very lack of resources and opportunities that forced these families to establish healthy relationships. When you aren't distracted with a multitude of things that separate your family throughout the day, you are forced to learn to reconcile conflicts, respect differences between people, and learn to enjoy another's company!

Chapter Fifteen

SURVIVAL OF THE ADAPTABLE

As an adult, no one ever asks you when you learned to read. It doesn't matter.

My second son Luke began his phonics career at age seven, following in the curriculum path of his older brother, Ben. Age seven went by, age eight, age nine, and still Luke wasn't reading. And we were using intensive, systematic, direct instruction phonics, for crying out loud! Tensions ran high, and the relationship between mom and son was suffering. Frequently Chris would come home from work to find Luke in tears or me in tears, or both of us in tears. This was not what we dreamed of for our homeschool! Chris asked me, "Does Luke enjoy *anything* about school?"

"Well," I said, "Luke likes it when I read to him." Chris had us stop everything else, and I just read aloud to Luke. Just read aloud. Nothing else! We sat on the floor, he hung upside down over the couch, we sprawled on the bed, and I read to him – great stuff, high interest boy stuff. We read books far beyond what a nine-year-old would normally read. This went on for six months! Our relationship did a lot of healing during that time. The stress was gone, and we were both ready to try again. Try again we did. We tried until we found a method that clicked. All of a sudden, the lights went on and Luke jumped right up to speed. What would have taken a six- or seven-year-old a year or so to learn, he flew through.

About three months after Luke began reading, we did standardized testing with the boys (crazy, I know!), and Luke tested ahead several grade levels in all subjects, even reading. But his test scores aren't the point of the story. They were simply an encouragement to us that he was fine. The point of the story is that our relationship had healed, and a young boy had been able to progress at his own pace, in his own way, and hadn't learned to hate reading! Had we not kept in our minds our ultimate goal of a lifelong learner, we would have seriously messed up and turned him off reading altogether. As an adult, no one ever asks you when you learned to read. It doesn't matter. The only concern is can you read? Furthermore, the kids who began reading at very early ages end up at the same place as the later readers. They're readers.

It was only after the fact that we realized that Luke is dyslexic. It runs in my family, and two more sons, along with Chris, are dyslexic. All we knew at the time was to keep trying different things until we found the right method that clicked with his learning style. He also benefited from a gain in maturity. Maturity does not cure dyslexia, but struggling students in general, especially little boys, can benefit from the gift of time. He needed the right timeline as much as the right curriculum. It is hard to go against the flow, but sometimes we must.

Chapter Sixteen

SLOW DOWN! CHILDREN AT PLAY!

Why can't kids be kids? What's the hurry? Are we afraid to let our children have a moment when they aren't engaged in some worthwhile, life enhancing activity? Sometimes the most valuable thing a kid can do is swing in the backyard, head thrown back, gazing at the sky. If we are filling all of their moments with things to make them well-rounded individuals, we might just be distracting them from discovering who they are created to be. Quiet and slow are not bad. Having nothing to do isn't bad. Boredom isn't necessarily bad. I've heard it said that life is full of boring moments. This will be good practice.

Tell me why a kid can't just show up and play little league baseball anymore. Why does a kids' sport now have to consume three or more nights a week and every weekend for six months? Why does my little sweetie have to have expensive uniforms and individual coaching just to play centerfield? I'm not sure it's wise to make everything in a child's life seem of such great importance. We might be sending the wrong message and creating entitled, self-absorbed adults.

> ## As parents, we need to be the boss of our own family!

Resist the tendency to think that your children need to excel in everything because they are being homeschooled, in order that your choices will be validated by their success! Be courageous and let them excel where they will excel and be average where they will be average. Sure we should encourage our kids to pursue their special talents. But if we're honest, I think we all know what I mean by relaxing about the whole performance issue. When I talk with parents about this topic, almost without exception they agree with me that there is just too much pressure in kids' activities. They dislike the time commitments, expense, and endless competition, but since they rarely change their children's activities to be in line with what they *say* they believe, I'm left to wonder. Perhaps we're afraid to be the one who doesn't take it so seriously because then the other kids will out-perform our kids. (That's likely to happen, too.) It's up to us to be the adult and say, "No, we're not going to come to soccer games from 7:30 a.m.–4:00 p.m. every Saturday. Furthermore, we're not going to allow our children to practice several hours each night, multiple nights of the week, and the expensive uniforms? Nope."

Do the math about the cost of all your family's activities – the time cost. You can earn money again. You can never get back your family's time. As parents, we need to be the boss of our own family! Stop letting sports teams, music lessons, church activities, debate clubs—you name it—dictate how you spend your lives. This isn't a dress rehearsal that we get to do over. Use time wisely, and don't be driven by what others are doing. Pick the things that add to your family, not drain it.

You might be surprised at what God does when we stick to our goals. The year our oldest son Ben graduated from our homeschool high school in May, he wasn't certain what he wanted to do. He stayed home, took classes at the local community college, and worked as a waiter in a restaurant. Come September, he decided that he'd like to go to Kings Point, the U.S. Merchant Marine Academy. This requires congressional nomination, as well as an appointment to the Academy. There's lots of paperwork and interviews, and that means it requires time! It was a bit late in the game to be starting the process. Additionally, upon examining his transcript, we realized we'd forgotten to prepare him for entrance to a federal academy! Instead of being involved in multiple sports and activities where he could demonstrate leadership that would earn him nice commendations for his transcript, we had chosen to pursue other things. Academies like participation in sports. We wanted our kids to participate in physical activities that they could continue into their adult lives, as well as something they could do together. Since Chris is a sailor, that's what we chose.

For several summers, Ben and his brothers competed in the youth sailing circuit. He had some wins and ended up with an above average record, but not by much. We hadn't pursued coaching for him, and we didn't live close to the water. He only sailed a few times a month, whereas the champion sailors had coaches and sailed almost every day. We knew that with a coach and more frequent sailing he would have been more successful, but it just wasn't a price we were willing to pay. What would the Academy think? They look for strong leadership in sports and other extracurricular activities, and Ben didn't have any. He hadn't participated in anything where he could show leadership skills.

However, during his last two years of high school, Ben had volunteered at a therapeutic horseback-riding center. Once again, this was a choice made because of our family and goals. Since our daughter Hannah has Down syndrome, she would be riding there. It was a natural place for the boys to serve, and service was an area that was important to us. You should also know that it was only when he could drive himself and his younger brother that this began. I still had little ones, and it would have been too chaotic for me to be shuffling them back and forth.

We scrambled to get it all together and sent in his information to our Congressmen and the Academy. It didn't look promising. Was God able to direct Ben's life given the choices we had made, or had we cost him an incredible opportunity? Was God able to get him into Kings Point, when we hadn't been specifically preparing for that for four years? As a matter of fact, as we all know, God was able. He was also willing, in this instance.

As a side note to Ben's acceptance into King's Point, we had the opportunity after his admission to visit with one of the Congressmen who nominated him for an appointment. He remembered Ben because of those volunteer hours. He told us that while he reviews applications of captains of football teams, honor society members, debate club members, and class presidents, he rarely sees volunteer hours. That impressed him enough to give Ben a nomination. He saw something unique and valuable in those hours. Believe it or not, Ben received a nomination to Kings Point from every Congressman he contacted. He also received a second nomination from one of them to the Naval Academy, and he hadn't even requested it! Trust God's leading for your family. Be bold and courageous enough to act on it.

Chapter Seventeen

HOMESCHOOL WITHOUT LOSING YOUR FAMILY

Homeschooling isn't rocket science, but it's not easy. Being responsible for the education of your children is a huge undertaking and one that shouldn't be entered into lightly. If we don't tend to family relational health as well, we can do damage over the long haul. Let's talk about some of those relational as well as practical issues that affect the smooth running of a home.

First and foremost, husbands and wives need to be in complete agreement about the decision to homeschool. It's okay to have a bit of insecurity, but I'm talking about when one spouse is completely opposed to the idea. I've never met a mom who was forced by her husband to homeschool. I've met plenty who were intimidated at the prospect, but their husband was sold on the idea. So the wife agreed to give it a try. That's not what I'm talking about here. Too often, a mom will tell me that her husband isn't on board with the decision to homeschool, but she badgered him into doing it because she just *knew* it was the right thing for their kids.

The method of home education may in fact be right for the kids, but I disagree with this scenario. When Dad isn't crazy about the idea, he probably feels he has valid reasons for being hesitant. If this was true in your case, then ideally you have already dealt with those concerns before beginning to homeschool. Everything doesn't have to be perfect before you start, but we need to at a minimum honestly address the issues. Instead, what usually happens is that Dad lets his wife wear him down, and he agrees to this homeschool thing. But Mom is on trial. The moment things get rocky, he decides that the difficulty proves his point that it wasn't a good idea. Now there is additional marital conflict in the home. Dad, you should have had the guts to just say "No" in the first place, rather than allow the disruption to your family.

Mom, if your husband has questions about your ability to homeschool, he might be right! He might be concerned about your ability to handle it physically. Maybe you've just had a difficult pregnancy and birth, already have lots of little ones at home, and things are chaotic. Maybe you have a demonstrated challenge with running a household with the kids in a regular school setting where someone else is responsible for delivering the content, and he is worried about your ability to run a household and get the kids' school done, too. There could be any number of reasonable, valid concerns. Let me remind you that this is the man who loves you and your children and wants what is best for everyone! And when the person who loves you most has concerns about something this important, you owe it to yourself to hear them out.

If you feel that God has put it on your heart to homeschool your children and your husband doesn't have a justifiable reason to disagree, I suggest you take it up with God. He is well able to change your husband's heart in His timing, which we know is always perfect. Trust God. If this scenario sounds familiar and you're several years into homeschooling, I still suggest that the two of you commit to seeking God on the issue so that you will be in agreement going forward. If you "win" the argument with your spouse over whether you will homeschool your children, you have both lost. You and your husband are one flesh, and you are fighting against yourself. You will damage your relationship if you continue in conflict. Work toward reconciliation so that everyone is on the same team, focused on the same end goal – the good of your family.

> *The health of the husband-wife relationship is the basis for your children's security.*

You've heard the admonition to nurture your relationship with your spouse because one of these days the kids will be gone. That's only partially true. We need to nurture our relationship with our spouse because our children are present right *now*, watching! The health of the husband-wife relationship is the basis for their security. People need a secure attachment system in order to learn and thrive. While in our homes, our children are watching us and learning how husbands and wives interact and serve one another. They are learning how mature adults resolve conflicts. They are learning how husbands and wives navigate trials. We can't be merely two adults living in the same house because mom is devoting all of her attention to schooling the kids. We moms can try to claim the moral high ground: "I'm educating our children, and I don't have time or energy to devote to my husband right now. His turn will come later." This is a false moral high ground. It's unwise and it isn't God's plan for families. It's just a feeble excuse. Furthermore, would we be okay if our husbands said, "I'm building my career, and I don't have time or energy to devote to my wife right now. Her turn will come later?" Parents, in the family your primary relationship focus is toward your spouse!

For most families, the wonderful thing that dads contribute to the homeschool is that they go to work each day so mom can stay home and educate the kids. Let's let dad off the hook if he's not holding family devotionals first thing in the morning before he leaves for work. Let's extend grace if he's not doing science experiments with the kids when he gets home at night. In all our years of homeschooling, I can probably count on one hand the number of dads who were able to consistently teach a subject to the kids or otherwise be practically involved in their homeschool. It just didn't work with working all day, too. They may have wanted to, but then reality stepped in. It's not a matter of both parents contributing equal time to the venture. You're on the same team, and you each contribute in different ways. Don't keep score as if you were opponents.

If I sound like I'm coming down too hard on the moms, it's because I'm telling you what I've seen and heard over almost three decades of doing this. If we know where the pitfalls are, we can avoid them. I want to give you a heads up that will enable your family to joyfully pursue this journey together.

Chapter Eighteen

TO TRAIN, OR NOT TO TRAIN, THAT IS THE QUESTION

I mentioned earlier that when we started homeschooling, we were given two very wise pieces of advice. You recall that the first one was to check your parental pride at the door. The second was to get your discipline in order. (Checking your parental pride at the door is vital in the area of parenting and discipline as well – not only just as it applies to academics and activities!) By that, they meant every area of parenting – filling your kids' emotional tanks, proactively teaching your children the behavior you expect from them, deciding on consequences for not behaving properly, and consistently carrying out the consequences. If you and I expect our families to enjoy this time of homeschooling, we aren't going to want to spend our days fighting with our kids to get them to obey and sit down to school!

Talk with your spouse and decide how you're going to get your children to do what you say. It's kind of hard to teach a child if you can't get them to do what you say! Our goal should be immediate, cheerful, full obedience. Homeschooling requires time and focus. If our home is in chaos due to a lack of good training in habits and behaviors, it's not conducive to learning anything. It will be exhausting and exasperating if your entire school day sounds like this, "Johnny, I said sit down. Johnny, sit down. I said sit down. It's time to do your schoolwork. Don't make me come over there. Johnny, sit down!"

Do your research. Read a whole book about parenting, not just a few blog posts. Better yet, read several books with varying ideas of teaching your children to obey. Once you decide what you're going to do, implement it! Just like in dieting, if you don't lose weight because you didn't follow the diet, the problem is with you and not the diet. This will be an investment of time in the beginning if you haven't already taught your children to do what you ask without drama, pouting, whining, and complaining. It will be time well spent, and will make life flow much more smoothly. I highly recommend that if you are pulling older children out of a conventional school setting, you get this in order before trying to begin serious academics. You'll more than make up for any time lost by doing this first.

One of my primary benchmarks for determining if my kids are on the right track toward maturity is whether they can control themselves. This has all kinds of implications. Can they keep random thoughts to themselves, or do they need to say everything that comes into their heads? It's quite a valuable life skill to exercise restraint in speaking. In some situations our words distract others – like in church, for instance, or when you're working with another child on math. Have our kids learned to keep their mouths closed until a more acceptable time comes when they can talk? Practicing self-control will allow them to push themselves a few more minutes until lunchtime, rather than plummeting into fits of anguish over their stomach growling. Practicing self-control will help them diligently finish their schoolwork, even though their friends and siblings are already outside playing, and they want to be out there, too. Self-control keeps us from doing all kinds of dumb things. If we use our time with our kids wisely, we can prepare them well to go out into the world and not be at the mercy of their flesh.

Chapter Nineteen

MOMS AND BOYS, OR CHECK YOUR FEMINISM AT THE DOOR

Culture is waging a war on males

Ladies, if we're homeschooling with an end goal in mind, and we want to effectively teach and influence our kids, we need to address an elephant in the room – culture is waging a war on males. It's currently fashionable to promote the idea that all males are bad and are to blame for most if not all of society's ills. The truth is that for males and females alike we can find plenty who are good, bad, wise or foolish. Today's media, which drives culture, seems committed to portraying men as irresponsible fools, incapable of handling the most basic of tasks, and clueless until the female in their life arrives to save them. Tragically, we've now targeted the boys in our world with these same allegations, even in Christian circles. With a house full of them, I'll admit that my viewpoint is skewed male. And, I *like* them! For the record, my boys are all *that* kind of boy - snakes, dirt

MOMS AND BOYS, OR CHECK YOUR FEMINISM AT THE DOOR

(preferably the wet kind), sweat, occasional goofiness, wrestling, rubber dog poop, fake roaches, and plastic vomit. You name it, that's them. They're also becoming gentlemen with courage, honor, and integrity. They're growing into men who are willing to take risks when necessary and lead in the face of uncertainty. And now, two are daddies who are devoted to their families, protect their wives and children, and sacrifice for those they love. Yes, they're good men, all.

Moms, we are our children's primary influence for large portions of the day. I want to remind us that as followers of Christ we cannot jump on the man-bashing bandwagon currently in vogue in our culture. In order to positively influence our sons as well as help them to learn, it is imperative that we communicate our respect for their male qualities. According to Shaunti Feldhahn in *For Women Only*, men equate respect with love. That's one reason Ephesians 5:33 instructs men to love their wives and women to respect their husbands (who happen to be male)! Remember that studies indicate we learn in positive ways only in a healthy attachment system when we feel loved and secure. As Christian mothers, it is our job to embrace and elevate God's creation of differences between males and females. This is a vital part of your homeschooling because if your boys don't see that you have respect for them, you're going to have a hard time teaching them. Let them be boys, and purpose to *like* them, not just love them.

I'd like to suggest two simple ways to show your sons that you respect them. According to Michael Gurian in *The Minds of Boys*, boys demonstrate care and affection with one another by rough and tumble wrestling, friendly smacks to the back, an impromptu arm wrestling match, or the ever popular *who can squeeze the hardest when you shake hands* greeting. It is noteworthy that we should be observing laughter and smiles during this process. If not, it's not the healthy interaction we're looking for. Culture says we should worry about this "violent" behavior. In fact, allowing boys to engage with their friends in this manner actually is a healthy form of male bonding. Girls will sit around, chat, and do one another's hair or fingernails. Boys want to karate chop one another! Let's be sure to pay attention to *everything* that is going on in the situation, and if there is laughter from *all* the boys, let them nurture their friendships. A standing rule in our house is that if everyone isn't having fun, then it isn't fun, and it stops.

I recall looking out my window one day to see three of my sons and two neighborhood boys wrestling in the front yard. One was hanging from another's neck. The other two were piled on top of a third lying in the grass. There was lots of laughter and smiles. I'm sure folks driving by were aghast at what was taking place in my yard, but I saw healthy play. The older boys were careful not to hurt the younger ones because they all knew that I was watching, and the younger ones loved the attention of the older boys. It reminded me of a bunch of puppies tussling, biting, pulling, and playing with their littermates! It's not hard to determine if you have healthy play happening or someone is getting beat up. If they race out the door to play with one another, it's good!

The second simple way we communicate respect for our sons is to edify their dad. Even young boys identify themselves as men, not boys. They learn how Mom views men by how she treats Dad. You edify their dad by acknowledging what a great father he is and how hard he works at his job so you have the privilege of staying home with them. You elevate manhood when you thank him in the presence of your kids for the way he serves your family. When I choose to speak highly of their dad in front of him and them, everyone wins! In the practical realm, the boys learn that being a good man earns the gratitude of others, and they will work to earn that for themselves. The boys learn what women view as valuable characteristics in a man, and they will seek to develop those characteristics. Proverbs 14:1 says, "The wise woman builds her house, but the foolish tears it down with her own hands," NASB (one assumes by her words, as well.) I want to build my house by speaking words that demonstrate my respect for the qualities of the males in my home. Do we not purposefully speak affirming words for our daughters? Would we give our sons anything less?

Chapter Twenty

SET PINTEREST ASIDE

Remember that if we're in this for the long haul, we need to periodically evaluate ourselves to be sure we're not sabotaging our own efforts! Let me reassure you that this is only a season in our lives. If we have a bunch of kids, it might be a long season, but it isn't forever! We won't always be homeschooling our children, and when we're finished, we can have back our perfectly imagined lives. Until that time, however, our families will survive and so will we.

While we're on this homeschool journey, some of us need to let go of our ideals of homekeeping that are no longer realistic with people in our house 24/7, working, eating, playing, and learning! This is the time to take a break from visions of the Pioneer Woman and Pinterest. Perfect life is for another season, unless perfection is an effortless venture for you. Time is a limited commodity; we might want to choose what gives us the most bang for the buck.

Let's address meals first. In the beginning, decide with your spouse what is the acceptable *minimum* standard for family meals. You may decide that merely having an adequate quantity of food on the table to keep starvation at bay is fine while you're getting yourself into the swing of things. Go with that until you feel you can add in more interesting variety. On the other hand, you may be a family of foodies, and meals are very important. You're going to have to figure out how to deliver that within the confines of your available time. I suggest simplifying it. Decide on three or four weekly menus that everyone likes and you can easily prepare. As a side note here, it is extremely helpful to teach your family to eat the same thing! It is possible. Prepare shopping lists for those menus, listing every single item required. That way you don't have to look up the recipes and compile a list each time you go shopping. Just check off what you need before going to the store. Then rotate those weekly menus. As you get used to your new schedule, add in more exciting things if you like. Until then, it's one less thing requiring a decision during the day. You'll have enough other things to keep your mind occupied.

I'm a very organized, neat, clean freak. I'm weird. I like to clean. But in order to survive, I've had to let go of ~~some~~ most of that! Left to my own devices, I'm not the mom who worries what people will think if they drop in unexpectedly. I'm the mom who wears out herself and her family and spends her time unwisely trying to keep everything in order! It's impossible at some periods in life. It just is. Other moms agonize over what they believe others are thinking about the state of their homes. The truth is, more often than not, we're all thinking about ourselves and not others! Instead of striving to create Pinterest worthy moments that we post on social media, let's dial it back a notch and relax. I realize moms fall anywhere on the spectrum of order versus chaos in their homes. I'm the mom who gets so caught up in tasks that I forget to enjoy my kids. Other moms forget where they *put* their kids.

Somewhere in between is a reasonable balance that honors our individual personalities and still establishes orderly homes where we can function. As with the meals, the first thing to do is to sit down with your spouse and agree on a standard, a minimum standard, to manage expectations. Chris always tells me, "Never assume anything." Never assume that you are absolutely correct in what you just *know* your spouse wants if you haven't talked about it.

> ## *We are training future husbands and wives.*

Remember this: Proverbs 14:4 ESV "Where no oxen are, the manger is clean, but abundant crops come by the strength of the ox." Here's my application: Where no children are, the house is clean, but much blessing comes by allowing children to be children. Does this mean that we allow our kids to make a mess all day long and never bat an eye? No, but it does mean that we make allowances for the fact that there are people in our homes 24/7, and it won't always be picture perfect! We have to adjust our expectations to meet reality if we want to survive and thrive while we're homeschooling.

SET PINTEREST ASIDE

Spend the time teaching your kids how to help you maintain an acceptable level of order in your home. It pays big dividends. We trained our oldest three boys well. We invested a lot of time teaching them to run the house. They could take care of everything. A funny thing happened, though. They began to grow up and leave home! The younger batch of kids wasn't ready for full-blown maintenance because we hadn't invested as much time in training them. Their older brothers had been handling everything, so the younger crowd was mostly just responsible for their personal space, beds, and clothes. This was a big mistake! Teaching all your children to contribute to the maintenance of your home is a huge factor in being able to get the important stuff in life done. Even little ones can be a help.

Remember, the bigger picture here is that we are training future husbands and wives. Don't you want your sons and daughters to marry women and men who are capable of taking care of themselves? Just keep in mind that while this training is taking place and skills are maturing, you and I need to manage our expectations.

When Hannah was young, it was her chore to fold towels. Every towel was folded differently, some more wadded up than folded. This was not the way I liked it, you know, the *right* way. But she was doing the best she could. Let's face it, it's a huge help just to have clean towels available and in a closet! Over time, her skills improved. Now I could have insisted on it being done my way, which would have meant doing it myself. Instead, I chose to train her to do it to the best of her ability, and I relaxed my standards. At the end of the day, does it matter if all my towels are folded exactly the same and the folds all face the same way? It's funny how things turn out. Nowadays, if I should need to get in Hannah's drawers to find an article of clothing and I mess up her perfectly folded things, she will take them *all* out and refold them all "properly." Apparently, I don't do it to suit her. Go figure.

Mom, perhaps your situation is different. Perhaps you're the less orderly one and your husband desires more order for your home than you feel is necessary. First, you need to ask yourself, "Is he right? Are we living in dirty, messy chaos? Are guests safe from the plague in my bathroom?" If he is right, then you owe it to him and your family to reach a realistic, sustainable standard on which you can both agree. Then *you* be willing to make the change. This could be one of those areas where God is going to grow you through the mundane things of life! This is not about having a perfect home. It's okay to be less than perfect, but we are trying to accomplish a lot in our homes every day. Is the state of our home working against that goal? Agree on that standard, work as a team, and teach the kids to help.

Don't confuse the big picture with the small picture. The state of your home is not the goal. The goal is to educate your children. In my case, I couldn't bear to start school until the house was in order. That usually meant that school started too late to accomplish things, or never started at all because, of course, you know there's a magic cut off time after which you simply *can't* start school. Something had to change, and I was it! For us parents, homeschooling is often about death to self. God uses it to change and grow us into more flexible, mature people. There are excellent resources full of ideas for getting your home life in order. Find the system that suits you, and get going. If the first one you try doesn't work in your situation, try another, and another, until you find one! Take baby steps, but keep taking them.

Chapter Twenty One

A Day in the Life

What does a real day in the life of a veteran homeschooling mom look like? Has she got it all figured out perfectly? How about a brief look at the memorable beginning of school a few years back? Let's check in again with Mom (me) and see how things are going. The plan was to begin on the first Tuesday of September. Sounds harmless, right? Tuesdays are good for school, and Tuesday mornings are even better. But this Tuesday morning, bright and early at 7:00 finds Mom trying to hustle 12-year-old Seth to the bathroom before he throws up on the floor. Seth proceeded to throw up about every 15 minutes or so throughout the entire day. Okay, maybe we don't start school Tuesday. Wednesday will be better. It's co-op day. That should be fun.

Wednesday morning bright and early, Hannah and Dad (Chris) headed off to her orthodontist appointment with plans to bring her to co-op when they finished. Big brother Ben happened to be home from work. Seth stayed home with him since Ben had been sick already. Gavin and Jack were enjoying their first day at co-op, and Hannah arrived about an hour before it ended. She ate a bit of lunch and began complaining that her stomach hurt.

A DAY IN THE LIFE

Mom, in all her experience and wisdom assumed that Hannah was probably just still hungry, but her teeth hurt from just having had her braces adjusted.

Classes ended at co-op and everyone piled into the truck to go home. About five minutes from home, Hannah began to throw up INSIDE the truck. Mind you, this was not the old van with plastic everything. This was the nice, newer truck with fancy leather interior. Mom wasn't quick enough to get the window down in time, so round one went inside the truck, down the window, and collected in that molded plastic thing at the bottom of the door where you store stuff – like umbrellas, with lots of fabric folds to hold liquid material. Not to worry, round two (and three) went outside (mostly) the truck, as Mom had reached over and shoved Hannah's upper body out of the window. Hannah threw up about every 15 minutes or so for the rest of the afternoon and evening.

Okay, some academically valuable stuff was accomplished at co-op. So while the start of the new school year was delayed a day, it wasn't a total loss. Wednesday night arrived and you guessed it. Gavin and Jack started throwing up, literally every 15 minutes like clockwork. Now here's the good part. The long-standing agreement in the house is that Dad does blood and guts and Mom does poop and vomit. Even though if you do the math, Dad comes out way ahead (there being only three incidents of stitches in 36 years of marriage and 7 kids), this plan has worked well. If Dad attempts to clean up poop or vomit, he has violent dry heaves, thus violating Rule #14 of *The 21 Rules of This House* – "We do not create unnecessary work for others." (You <u>must</u> check out *The 21 Rules of This House* by Gregg and Josh Harris at www.dohardthings.com! Really, stop and do it right now, but do come back. You don't want to miss anything.) If Mom tries to handle blood and guts, she violates the unwritten, but non-negotiable rule of the house "Mommy doesn't pass out and hit her head on the floor."

In an effort to protect the newly replaced carpet in the boys' room, Gavin and Jack were moved onto the hardwood floor of Mom and Dad's bedroom. Of course, this was done under the guise of having them closer to a bathroom toilet. Mom and Dad made them little sleeping pallets and equipped them with their own trashcans in which to throw up. When Gavin started heaving, Mom jumped out of bed and rushed him to the bathroom. Dad (who is also moved to throw up if he has to even *listen* to others throwing up and has been outside the bathroom door with his fingers in his ears) came in and disinfected after them.

After Gavin was settled on his pallet again, Jack started heaving. Mom jumped out of bed and rushed Jack to the bathroom, where he put his brother to shame. Again, Dad was poised outside the door, germ killers in hand, waiting for the "all clear" to enter. Mom got Jack all cleaned up and onto his pallet, climbed into bed, slept for about five minutes, and Gavin was up again. At about 2 a.m., Dad was no longer standing guard outside the bathroom door. Mom assumed he couldn't take it anymore and was leery of contributing to the problem. Finally, 6:00 a.m. rolled around, and the fits of vomiting had slowed to every 30 to 45 minutes. Dad dragged himself out of bed and said to Mom, "Isn't it great that you got a four-hour break from them throwing up? They must be getting better!" He had fallen asleep and not known that this had been going on ALL NIGHT LONG! Mom forgets the accurate account of who was the next to fall victim to this oh-so-nasty bug, but suffice it to say that everyone in the house got it. Mom was so weak from no sleep and caring for sick kids—and being sick herself and up all night—that they couldn't do anything valuable until Wednesday, co-op day, the next week.

That Thursday was spent preparing for Hurricane Ike – the first hurricane in about 25 years to make a direct hit on Houston. Ike hit Friday night, and the family spent the next 10 days without power, cleaning up debris, and playing in the mud. A few days they tried to do a little school (the weather was unseasonably cool for most of that time, so there was no valid excuse other than the total disruption of life), but not much was accomplished. If you're keeping up, it's three weeks into the first month of the plan for the school year, and things aren't looking good. Surely, the fourth week will be better....

Monday morning of the fourth week dawned with a brand new addition to the schedule – Hannah started her period for the first time. This was uncharted territory for Mom, but she had already asked other moms with mentally handicapped girls how they handled it. They all recommended a schedule of frequent trips to the bathroom. No problem, Mom had nothing else to do with her day! By Wednesday, though, Hannah and Mom had a good system going, so some real school was completed that week! It took nearly a month to get the first week of school done!

I recount the continuing drama of Mom and Dad to remind us all that while it is wise to make plans, we also need to remain flexible and maintain a sense of humor. I look back on it now, and it makes me laugh. It is reassuring to know that God is always with us, even when our plans go awry.

Chapter Twenty Two

DON'T GIVE UP THE SHIP

Sometimes we ask another homeschooling mom about her homeschool. She tells us what she's doing, and it seems much more academically challenging than what we are doing with our children. We look at her and believe she's got it all together. Her kids appear to be so smart, and the curriculum appears to be one that will deliver *the* academic program to our children. I have no doubt that she appears to have it all together, her curriculum is excellent, and that her children are smart. I would encourage you to remember, however, that often we don't get the whole story.

Folks rarely tell us that each day ends in tears of frustration, mom and kids. Neither do they share their feeling of isolation from real relationship with their kids. If we're quizzing a mom whose kids are older, she's not likely to tell us that her children left home as soon as they could, want nothing to do with the family, want nothing to do with learning for pleasure, and would never consider homeschooling their own children. People rarely confide that the stressful pace of their life causes them or their children health problems. I say "Big deal" if our kids get perfect SAT scores. "Big deal" if they get into the most prestigious colleges. "Big deal" if they have a high paying job. If the price to obtain those things is poor relationships, poor health, no joy, and no peace, then I say "No thanks." To me, if that's all there is to show for my effort at the conclusion of our homeschool journey, I have failed. Relationships and character are the real prizes.

I've said before that an academically rigorous education and good relationships and character aren't mutually exclusive. However, if the pursuit of that achievement costs us our families, then we're making a poor choice in pursuing it. Neither am I saying that pursuing the things that truly matter, keeping in step with our goals, guarantees us perfect families. At some point, our kids grow up and make their own choices. We can, however, stack the deck in our favor by not turning them away from us by our incessant need to impress all those around us.

When it's all said and done, will we wish we had diagrammed more sentences or that we'd sat on the couch and read with our children? Sometimes the wisest thing we can do is recognize that we are drowning in a flood of *too much* – too much stuff, too much running around, too much academic load, too much! We need to plug the hole and stop the flood. It's possible that our decision might let someone down. It's also possible that our actions will inspire another family to take back their lives. We wear out our families and ourselves by doing more than what we're supposed to be doing. It's as if we get personal fulfillment by being the busiest person on the block. I'm sure there's no extra crown in heaven for the busiest person on the block.

Let's play "What If...." I chew on this scenario myself, and I don't know the answer. Indulge me if you will. What if, after much prayer, we make our plans for our homeschool according to the individual bent of each child? What if my seven year old, when asked what he does for fun, what sports he plays, answers, "I like plumbing"? What if I spend extra dollars on pipes, and fittings, and nozzles, and hoses, and let him go to town creating things in our back yard? What if at the library, instead of typical kid books, he checks out *Plumbing 1-2-3* and pores over it?

What if his passion lasts over the next few years? What if I let him study all about plumbing, and since time is limited, we don't learn to write Haiku poetry, and he can't state a single fact about the history of the Ming dynasty? But he can fix any plumbing problem we have, and he finds purpose and joy in stopping leaks, fixing clogged things, and designing drainage systems?

When I ponder this, I find that the most difficult part about it is totally letting go of the accepted scope and sequence and just choosing to follow a kid's passion. I know that this is what an un-schooling family does, but we don't typically think of ourselves as such. Frankly, I admire their courage! We seem to labor under the fear that when our children grow up they won't be able to support themselves. But we don't know if that's the case since so few of us have the courage to try it. Anyhow, it's worthy of speculation. How many adults do you know who are actually still working in a field related to what they studied in college? If they are, how many of them wish they were doing something else and hadn't chosen a path because that's where all the good jobs were. Are they still in that job because it provides security, rather than enjoyment? The golden handcuffs. Of course, there is not going to be excitement and passion in every moment of life because if everything were extraordinary, then the extraordinary would be ordinary. But what would our society look like if most folks were working in areas they actually enjoyed?

Direction from God is never a matter of public opinion.

I see new homeschooling families choosing an educational methodology that requires so much effort on mom's part that there's virtually no way she'll be able to carry that load for the long haul. Perhaps in the short term, it makes us feel confident to choose that which requires so much of us. Maybe we reason that if it's difficult, it must be good, so we force our kids to tackle much more than is necessary or appropriate for their age or ability. And we force ourselves to force them because we believe it's the only way they will be properly educated. But if all this effort leaves no energy for attending to the most important things—relationships and the character of our kids—then we've made a poor choice, even if everyone else is making the same choice.

I love this passage from *Let Go of Whatever Makes You Stop* by John Mason. "If a thousand people say a foolish thing, it is still a foolish thing. Direction from God is never a matter of public opinion. A wise man makes his own decision; an ignorant man follows public opinion. Don't think you're necessarily on the right road because it's a well-beaten path."[2]

I'm not impressed if my child can logically and persuasively argue the theological position of the eternal security of the believer if he lacks the personal self-discipline to get up off the couch and offer to help around the house. There's nothing wrong with intellectual excellence, but there comes a time when our personal witness, born out of what folks see actually happening in our lives, gets in the way of what comes out of our mouths, however profound it may be. I'm seeing homeschooled graduates these days who readily spout off facts and figures, name places on maps and empires won and lost, recite wonderful Bible verses from memory, yet are completely lacking in self-control, show profound disrespect to their parents, and are generally most unpleasant to be around because they whine, pout, and complain. Mom sits nearby, completely spent due to all her efforts pursuing academic superiority and achieving the well-rounded child through activities, oblivious to the missing character component. Parents, we must do better than that!

---

2   Mason, *Let Go of Whatever Makes You Stop*, p. 58.

Chapter Twenty Three

ABUNDANT LIFE HOMESCHOOLING

A few years back we decided that the goal for the coming school year was to refocus on family relationships and joy in our home. I wanted to enjoy my kids without seeing an expiration date stamped on their foreheads. After much prayer and discussion, Chris and I developed a plan for the year with specifics about how we wanted to incorporate activities and the curriculum that would facilitate a more relaxed, joyful environment for all of us. We committed it to paper. Then I made a bad decision and watched a webinar for a particular curriculum – not the one Chris and I had chosen.

I don't know if you've seen the old animated film *The Jungle Book*. It's a great film, by the way, sweet and charming and funny. There's this scene where the character of Kaa, the boa constrictor who wants to eat the child Mogli, is coiled up in a tree. Mogli is in the tree as well, and Kaa engages him in conversation. Before Mogli realizes it, he's been captured by Kaa's hypnotic spinning eyes and is on his way to becoming dinner!

I, too, was about to become dinner, hypnotized by the promise of excellence that this curriculum had to offer. The method was completely outside of the goals we had set for our homeschool, but (in endless discontent? fear? distraction?) I had kept looking (just to see what's out there, of course) and found myself caught in the trap! "Oh my, now THIS is nice!" When I suggested my sparkling new idea to Chris, he wisely shook me out of my stupor and reminded me of our goal and plan – the one that we had agreed on after much discussion and prayer! This was the plan whose function was to bring the joy back to our homeschool. Sometimes I dream of curriculum marketed under such terms as *"Joy," "Delight," "Poor Fit,"* or *"Unnecessarily Time Consuming."* The trouble is what brings heartache to one family is the perfect choice for another. Remember that our #1 job is to find God's direction for our family!

God has graciously delivered us from bondage to a system of education, one that despite the best efforts of dedicated and caring teachers can only be a one-size-fits-all method. Now that we have this freedom, what are we going to do with it? Does God break chains of bondage so we can enslave ourselves again? Leaving aside for a moment what your state laws might require of you academically, do you realize that the very fact that you are home with your children and influencing their lives is a Big Deal? We have been given this incredible opportunity to be with our children, spending time passing along God's truth in a way that just isn't possible if they are out of our homes eight or nine hours each day. We foolishly think that our main purpose is to ensure good grades and just get into college.

I like the story of God delivering the Israelites from bondage in Egypt. Many things in that story remind me of my family's journey in homeschooling. During their 400 years of slavery, God had a plan to deliver them by His great power in order to give them a land for their inheritance, a land where they would occupy, possess, and influence the people around them. He prepared Moses to be the one to carry the message. God worked many miracles on their behalf and ultimately changed Pharaoh's heart to let the people of Israel go free, and He gave them clear direction by a cloud during the day and pillar of fire at night. When they reached the Red Sea and saw Pharaoh's army coming after them, they cried out in terror and even wanted to go back to their old lives as slaves. God delivered them again in a miraculous way, and all six million or so of them walked through dry ground in the middle of the Red Sea.

Imagine all of the creative things God could have done here. He could have just wiped out the army and been done with it. He could have miraculously transported the Israelites to the other side in the blink of an eye, or He could have made the water solid for them to walk across – just as similar things happened to others in the Bible. To strengthen them, He chose to allow his people to be afraid and uncertain and watch His deliverance. Even after these magnificent demonstrations of God's care and leading, the Israelites still weren't satisfied and grumbled about their food. God provided daily sustenance to meet their needs.

When I compare that to our homeschool experience, I can see that God had a plan for His present day people to deliver them from bondage. If you're a new homeschool parent, you might not have any idea of the history and battle waged for the privilege to educate your children at home. Years ago, pioneer homeschoolers risked everything, including loss of their kids and jail time, to fight for our freedom to homeschool. Take a moment right now if you haven't ready, and join your state homeschool organization or write them a big fat check in support of their continuing efforts to maintain that freedom. Homeschooling is NOT a guaranteed right, as you may have comfortably assumed, but a currently legislated freedom subject to attack and change at any moment. The pioneer homeschool parents were our version of Moses, struggling with the government to let their children go.

God alone changes the hearts of kings; He alone changed the hearts of those in power to allow us this remarkable freedom. Even with so great a deliverance and the clear mandate from God in his Word to educate my family, just like the Israelites, I can still falter in fear of my circumstances. I will romanticize that yellow school bus cruising through my neighborhood, carrying children away to a place where someone else is directing their education, and my day is again my own. I battle with wondering if the standard way of doing things in traditional schools is better after all, if my kids are being shortchanged in some way. Often I just want to go back to the security of knowing that in a regular school setting, someone else is calling the shots. Someone else is responsible. It's on those occasions that I chafe against what God has clearly called us to do, and I long to just do what everyone else is doing and not worry about it. I want ease. And I get weak.

In the same way God sustained Israel with manna, He has generously supplied us with encouragement and support in the form of books, blogs, podcasts, and conferences, enough to fill us up to the full each and every day. And we, like Israel and the daily manna, have to go get it for ourselves.

But could it be that this idea of educating your own children, and not just educating your own kids but doing so in a way that might be a bit out of the norm, is the deliverance from a culture gone nuts? Could it be that this is bigger than your family and mine? Could God be telling another story of His glorious deliverance from bondage? Perhaps the challenging things are the very things that strengthen us in the same way that waiting on God's deliverance strengthened Israel. We have been given freedom to follow this different path, but it might not be what we've expected. We will have to let go of our long held views of success, comfort, and status.

Let's ask ourselves, "What is our personal Egypt, the thing that holds us back, keeps us in bondage?" I have a few possible answers. It could be loyalty to the idea that only one method is acceptable for our kids' education, even if it doesn't fit them well. In this way, we cling to the conventional, safe methods of school that we have always known. Do we want to go back to the same old one-size-fits-all education when there has never been a one-size-fits-all kiddo? Do we find safety in tradition or the promise of academic excellence offered by a particular method – even though it's not suited to our family?

Are we still in bondage to the opinions, either perceived or real, of our peers? You know, you're sitting with other homeschool moms and someone says, "What? Your children aren't beginning Latin instruction in 2nd grade? What? You're not participating in XYZ co-op? It's the most academically rigorous one out there. My Suzie scored in the 99th percentile on her SAT and has a full ride scholarship to Harvard. So, what's new with you? How are your kids doing?"

Or maybe what keeps us in bondage is our own fear of the future. What if our children don't get into college? What if they don't want to go to college? How will they ever get a job, have money, be happy? (Read: make me look like I did a good job.) What if our kids aren't as academically adept as others? What if someone finds out that our family is not what it appears to be, that my kids are average, my house isn't perfect, and sometimes we eat Fruit Loops instead of organic quinoa for breakfast? Let's ask ourselves what would happen if we chose to trust God's leading for our family, rested in it, and found abundant peace.

Trusting is hard, even when you've seen God deliver you and make good on his leading! Certainly the Israelites had seen God work miracles on their behalf, yet they still lacked peace. Having launched five of our kids out into the adult world and having seen God be faithful to bless the atypical path they took should give me great faith. (For the record, by *bless* I don't mean everything was easy and perfect. I mean that we can see that God is developing these men according to His plan, and He is molding them according to His good purpose.)

In John 10:10 ESV, we find Jesus' words, "The thief comes only to steal and kill and destroy; I came that they may have life and have it abundantly." I propose we ask ourselves what would happen if we choose abundant life for our homeschooling adventure. I think we believe it isn't possible to have abundant life in our homeschool. But Jesus said it is. He intended that we have it. Purpose to follow God's leading and let Him take care of the outcome. We are not called to victory, success, and comfort. We are called to obedience.

Trust what God is speaking to your heart

Let me encourage you with a look at the story of Jesus and the disciples found in Mark 4:35–41. Jesus had just healed the leper and many others, and He was tired. At His direction, the disciples got into a boat with Him and were crossing the Sea of Galilee. A fierce storm rose up, and water began filling the boat. These experienced sailors were afraid for their lives, and Jesus was asleep! In case you're unaware, if you're on a boat with seasoned sailors in a storm and *they're* afraid, you are truly in big trouble! Big trouble! Because these men knew that their situation was dire and Jesus seemed unaware, they thought that He didn't care, didn't see, and didn't understand.

When they woke him, He calmed the sea and said to the wind, "Peace, be still." And then to the disciples, He addressed these questions, "Why are you so timid? How is it that you have no faith?" Could those commands given to the sea and the wind—"Peace, be still"—also have been just a tiny bit for the disciples as well? I mean, when the creator of the universe gives instructions to creation, we'd all better pay attention!

Those words are also for our benefit when we're in the storms of homeschool life. The same Jesus who is King over the wind and the waves, the Lord over all creation, is Lord over our families, college scholarships, ADHD, struggling students, and parents who wonder if they're doing this thing right. I ask you this ... is your Creator saying to you, "Peace, be still. Why are you so timid? How is it that you have no faith?"

God has given us everything we need for life, and homeschooling! He has set us free to live abundantly. Live like those who have been set free. Trust what God is speaking to your heart about your family and children and your homeschool. Act on what He says, and then relax.

We've taken quite a trip together. I hope you have been challenged to dream significant things for your family and homeschool. I hope you won't be content with merely bringing school home, but that you have been inspired to create something entirely unique. Your kids deserve nothing less. You get one chance to profoundly and positively affect the trajectory of your children's lives. Do it well!

In closing, let me remind you of this: "If God doesn't build the house, the builders only build shacks. If God doesn't guard the city, the night watchman might as well nap. It's useless to rise early and go to bed late and work your wearied fingers to the bone. Don't you know he enjoys giving rest to those he loves? Don't you see that children are God's best gift? The fruit of the womb is his generous legacy. Like a warrior's fistful of arrows are the children of a vigorous youth. Oh, how blessed are you parents, with your quivers full of children! Your enemies don't stand a chance against you; you'll sweep them right off your doorstep." (Psalm 127, The Message) And this: When Moses died, and God was sending Joshua to lead the Israelites into the Promised Land, God said this to Joshua, "Have I not commanded you? Be strong and courageous. Do not be frightened, and do not be dismayed, for the Lord your God is with you wherever you go." Joshua 1:9 ESV

Bibliography

Feldhahn, Shaunti. *For Women Only: What You Need to Know about the Inner Lives of Men.* Colorado: Multnomah Books, 2004.

Gurian, Michael, and Patricia Henley. *Boys and Girls Learn Differently! A Guide for Teachers and Parents.* San Francisco: Jossey-Bass, 2001.

Mason, John. *Let Go of Whatever Makes You Stop.* Tulsa, Oklahoma: Insight International, 1994.

Tough, Paul. *How Children Succeed: Grit, Curiosity and the Hidden Power of Character.* London: Random House, 2012.

The 21 Rules of This House, www.dohardthings.com/21-rules-of-this-house.

Student Handouts, www.studenthandouts.com.

BIBLIOGRAPHY

Determining Children's Learning Styles
Fuller, Cheri. *Talkers, Watchers, and Doers: Unlocking Your Child's Unique Learning Style*. Colorado Springs: Piñon Press, 2004.

Koch, Kathy, PhD. *8 Great Smarts: Discover and Nurture Your Child's Intelligences*. Chicago: Moody Publishers, 2016.

Step by Step approach to goal setting
Hyatt, Michael, and Daniel Harkavy. *Living Forward: A Proven Plan to Stop Drifting and Get the Life You Want*. Grand Rapids, Michigan: Baker Books, 2016.

www.ingramcontent.com/pod-product-compliance
Lightning Source LLC
Chambersburg PA
CBHW071227090426
42736CB00014B/3000